La Palma

Klaus Wolfsperger
Annette Miehle-Wolfsperger

Walks on

La Palma

Translated by Tony Pearson

50 selected walks on the coasts
and in the mountains of the »Isla Bonita«

With 112 colour photographs,
49 walking maps with a scale of 1:50.000,
a walking map with a scale of 1:100.000 and
an overview map with a scale of 1:150.000

ROTHER · MUNICH

Front cover:
Volcanic landscape at the foot of Volcán Martín.

Frontispiece (photo on page 2):
In summer the high mountains display the full splendour of their flowers.
High walk on the Pico de la Nieve.

All photographs are by the authors, with the exception of the photos on
pages 70, 71 and 101 (Eberhard Wolfsperger).

Cartography:
Walking maps with a scale of 1:50.000 / 1:100.000 © Freytag-Berndt,
Vienna; Overview maps © Klaus Wolfsperger

Translation:
Tony Pearson

1st edition 2001
© Bergverlag Rother GmbH, Munich

ISBN 3-7633-4808-5

Distributed in Great Britain by Cordee, 3a De Montfort Street, Leicester
Great Britain LE1 7HD, www.cordee.co.uk
in USA by AlpenBooks, 3616 South Road, C-1, Mukilteo, WA 98275 USA,
www.alpenbooks.com

ROTHER WALKING GUIDES

Côte d'Azur · Crete West · Cyprus · Gran Canaria · Iceland · La Palma · Madeira ·
Mallorca · Mont Blanc · Norway South · Provence · Sardinia · Sicily · High Tatra ·
Tenerife · Tuscany North · Valais East · Around the Zugspitze

**Dear mountain lovers! We would be happy to hear your opinion
and suggestions for amendment to this Rother walking guide.**

BERGVERLAG ROTHER · Munich
D-85521 Ottobrunn · Haidgraben 3 · Tel. (089) 608669-0, Fax -69
Internet www.rother.de · E-mail bergverlag@rother.de

Preface

The greenest of the Canary Islands awaits the walker with such a variety of landscapes as can hardly be found in any other similarly small region in the world. Wide valleys, pine and laurel woods, banana plantations, rugged gorges and crater landscapes, cascades and waterfalls contrast with one another. The walking here is superb, and the dark-black beaches, beautiful as they are, pale into insignificance in comparison to the offerings of nature, which in all corners of the island surprise one with ever changing scenes. The island offers incomparable pleasant strolls between gleaming lava beaches, lush laurel woods and cloud-ringed ridges. And ever-present is the deep blue Atlantic.

La Palma is made for the walker who loves nature and seeks adventures away from the noisy beach resorts and cheap tourist attractions. This can be seen in the wide range of enjoyable recommended routes, which are offered to the walker. They meet all expectations and cover all areas of the »Isla Bonita«: from adventurous excursions into the rugged barrancos in the north to the romantic scenery of the setting sun from the 2000 metre peaks, to the volcanoes which top everything; from gentle walks through the open green pine forests and dark lava fields to the most spectacular walking destination on the island – the giant unspoilt landscape of the Caldera de Taburiente, surrounded by thousand metre high precipices, one of the greatest erosion craters in the world.

In this, the first English edition, numerous new walks, which were little known before, have been included, and most of the other recommended walks have been checked, improved and brought right up-to-date. However, changes can take place in the walks described, both as a result of continual natural processes and, of course, as a result of the intervention of people. Therefore we would ask you to send any corrections or suggestions to the publisher. We wish you an enjoyable and exciting holiday on this »island of eternal spring«.

Spring 2001   Klaus and Annette Wolfsperger

Contents

Tourist Information

Use of the Guide

The most important information for each of the suggested walks is summarised as a list of key points. After a short description of the main characteristics of the walk, a detailed route description is given. The coloured walking map with a scale of 1:50.000 has the route marked on it. All walking destinations, place names, starting and finishing points and all important points en route are listed in the index at the back of the book. Maps on the inner cover at the back and before the section with the walks give an overview of where the individual walks are situated.

Grade

Most of the walks follow distinct paths and tracks. One should not however be deceived by this as some of the routes require a good level of fitness, sure-footedness, a head for heights and a good sense of direction. One should be aware that routes can be much more difficult in unfavourable weather conditions. So that the difficulties of the suggested routes can be better assessed, the route numbers are colour-coded as follows:

BLUE   These walks follow paths which are generally reasonably wide and not too steep and can therefore be done with relatively little danger in poor weather.

RED   These walks follow paths which are generally narrow and can be exposed over short sections. They should therefore, only be undertaken by sure-footed mountain walkers. Short sections can also make considerable demands on navigation skills.

BLACK   These mountain walks are often narrow and steep. In places they can be very exposed, or where they cross steep slopes there may be a danger of slipping, but only seldom will scrambling actually be involved. This means that these routes are only suitable for sure-footed, mountain walkers who have a head for heights, are fit and have experience of proper mountain conditions. A good sense of direction is also required.

Dangers

Most of the walks follow clear and well-marked paths. In cases where sections of paths are especially exposed or demanding this is indicated in the text. On the mountain slopes and ridge tops (especially on the eastern side of the island) and particularly after midday, one has to take account of the trade wind clouds, which can result in thick fog and visibility below 10 metres. Often the clouds only disperse towards evening and they can cause considerable navigation difficulties for the mountain walker. Moreover on the ridge tops of Cumbres and the Caldera there is often a strong, gusty wind comparable to the Föhn wind in the Alps. After heavy rain barrancos

Ruta de los Volcanes

The most fascinating walk on La Palma: impressive volcano landscape and views (Walk 33; 6½ hrs).

Through the Caldera de Taburiente

The second show tour of the island: Los Brecitos – Playa de Taburiente – Barranco de las Angustias (Walk 37; 6¼ hrs).

Marcos y Cordero

From Los Tilos to Casa del Monte, on to the Cordero Spring and descent through the Barranco del Agua to Los Tilos (Walks 9, 8, 10; 7 hrs).

From La Zarza to El Tablado

Two fantastic completely different barrancos in one go (Walks 18 and 20; 5 hrs).

Pico Bejenado

The most beautiful panoramic summit on La Palma (Walk 41; 4 hrs).

Roque de los Muchachos

Caldera ridge walk with spectacular views (Walk 48, possibly in combination with Walk 45; 3¾ hrs / 5½ hrs).

Volcán Teneguía

From Fuencaliente through a lava landscape and vineyards to the youngest volcano in the Canaries (Walk 36; 5 hrs).

Las Tricias

Pleasant walk through a picture book village possibly with a descent to Puerto (Walks 21 and 22; 1¾ hrs / 6¼ hrs).

From Ermita Virgen del Pino to Refugio de la Punta de los Roques

Wonderful ascent with plenty of views to the refuge hut high above the Cumbrecita (Walks 29 and 42; 6 hrs).

From Barlovento to Gallegos

Rugged romantic barrancos and sleepy villages (Walk 15; 5¼ hrs).

and mountain slopes threatened by landslips should be avoided. Always stay on designated paths or the routes described, especially in the Caldera.

Equipment

Stout ankle-high shoes with a non-slip sole and tough trousers are required, sun cream and possibly sun hat, protective clothing against wind, rain and the cold as well as provisions for the walk (adequate liquid).

Walking times

Times given are for actual walking time and do not include time for rests or photos. In general times are given for the stages of the walk as well as the total time.

Food and accommodation

There are no huts with wardens on La Palma. The few refuge huts (refugio) serve at best as shelters or for emergencies and in some cases there is no access to them. Places for eating or accommodation are therefore mainly restricted to villages and towns. It is possible to obtain permission from the National Park authorities to put up a tent for one night on the campsite at the Playa Taburiente.

Approach

Many walks can be reached by public transport, but sometimes an approach by car is necessary. The bus timetable for the main traffic routes is to be found in front of the section with the walk descriptions. Further information about the approach is given with the individual walk description.

Best time of year

La Palma is an all-year-round walking destination. In the winter months (November to April) the weather is not as stable as in the summer. Snowfall down to 1500 metres and heavy showers of rain are not unusual at this time. In the warm, at times hot, high summer months it is recommended to avoid walks on the south side or near the coast.

Maps

The walking maps for the recommended walks with a scale of 1:50.000 or 1:100.000 are an essential part of the guide. For those who want to obtain an additional map, the Freytag-Berndt maps or the Kompass maps with a scale of 1:50.000 are to be recommended. The two part military maps with a scale of 1:50.000 and the eight-part map with a scale of 1:25.000 from the Instituto Geografico Nacional are also right up-to-date. However many walking paths are not indicated on these topographical maps.

Nature and the environment

Please respect all the plants and animals, take your rubbish back with you, do not carelessly throw away cigarette ends and avoid making open fires – forest fires, even on this relatively rain-rich island, are not uncommon.

Tips for long distance walkers

Many of the suggested walks are designed as long distance walks or staged walks where the end point is a long way from the start. Here it is recommended either to use public transport (bus, taxi) or to join up with an organised walking group (various organisers on the island: it is best to ask in hotels) or it is possible to join up with another motorised walker. It is best to park one car at the end of the walk or alternatively to swap car keys at some point on the walk and drive back with the other walker's car (clear previous arrangement necessary!)

Long-distance walkers have good opportunities for multi-day walks on La Palma. The Great Caldera circuit, following paths within the Caldera, is very worthwhile (base: campsite at the Playa de Taburiente), as is a traverse of the north of the island from Los Tilos/Los Sauces via Barlovento to Santo Domingo de Garafía (2–3 days). By making use of this guide it is also possible to put together other multi-day walks on La Palma.

Walking on La Palma

The greenest of the Canary Islands

San Miguel de la Palma, as the most northwesterly and fifth largest of the Canary Islands is known in its unabbreviated form, is of volcanic origin like the other islands in the Canary Archipelago. However, the lush vegetation and the richly contrasting landscapes distinguish it from the other more barren and less forested neighbouring islands. It is not a coincidence that the »Isla Verde« is known as the best Canary Island for walking. For despite its relatively dense population (just 90,000 inhabitants) the 726km² island has still got plenty of unspoilt nature – in the pine and laurel woods of the Cumbre as well as in the nature reserve of the Caldura de Taburiente, in the wilderness of gorges in the northern part of the island as well as in the ash fields in the south. The particular charm of the island arises from its contrasts. Dominating the heart-shaped island is the mighty erosion crater of the Caldera de Taburiente. This is surrounded by a mountain ridge, roughly 28km long and up to 2426m high, and which covers the whole of the north side of the island. It slopes down to a precipitous coast, mainly gently but cut into by numerous Barrancos. The south is characterised by the stretched out volcano chain of the Cumbre Vieja – this is of recent origin and the eye is drawn to numerous lava streams.

Typical island weather – clouds on the east side, sun in the west. View from Pico Birigoyo to Cumbre Nueva and the Caldera de Taburiente.

Flora and Fauna

The island has a number of completely different vegetation zones, dependant on the altitude and the climatic conditions. The flora is correspondingly varied with numerous endemics (plants which occur exclusively on the island). Undemanding xerophytes flourish along the coastal regions: dragon trees (especially in the north, sometimes groves with more than ten specimens) and palms are no rarity. Dominant however, are the succulents (spurge and cacti) and of course bananas, the most important economic product of the island. The intensively irrigated plantations subsidised by the state and the EU, cover large areas of the coastal region up to a height of about 300m. A good 40% of the island is covered by forest: the dense jungle-like laurel forest (sub tropical mountain forest) grows exclusively on the damp north and east facing slopes and gorges. In the rain-rich northeast this sometimes reaches almost to the coast. Above the laurel forest is the Fayal-Brezal zone (tree heaths and gale) and the sparsely wooded pine forest (on the western and southern slopes too). The Canary pine (Pinus canariensis) is very fire resistant and survives the most severe of forest fires. In the high areas over 2000 metres the landscape is dominated by the broom-like laburnum bushes which display their yellow flowers in spring and the Teide broom with its white flowers.

Found everywhere on the island – little natural wonders.

The only mammals which are frequently seen in the mountains are rabbits and rats. The number of wild goats and barbary sheep (Arruí) is impressive (in and around the Caldera de Taburiente) but one seldom gets to see them. The only poisonous animal is the millipede, which grows up to 10 cm long and which is exclusively found under stones. The bite of this rare arthropod is dangerous, even for people. Specialities in the bird world are the Laurel Pigeon and the wild canary.

Prehistoric rock etchings
La Palma possesses numerous finds of prehistoric rock etchings – drawings and inscriptions from the original inhabitants of the Canaries (the Guanches), which are chiselled into the rocks by pointed stones and even today have not been clearly deciphered. It is probable that the meaning of the mainly spiral and meander-shaped signs

Drago (dragon tree).

are connected with water, as most of the finds are at springs. Rock engravings have also been found in caves and ancient cult places. The most famous are the sites in the Cueva de Belmaco (Mazo, Visitor Centre), La Zarza/La Zarcita (Visitor Centre, see Walk 19) as well as La Fajana (near El Paso). Among the walks in this guide the following prehistoric rock etching sites are encountered: Buracas (Walk 21) Roque Teneguía (Walk 36) Tamarahoya (Walk 41) and La Erita (Walks 43–45, 50).

National Park (Parque Nacional Caldera de Taburiente)
The Caldera de Taburiente National Park was established in 1954, and in 1981 its final present day protective zone was determined (4690 ha). The erosion crater with a diameter of up to 8km is one of the mightiest and most impressive crater basins on the Earth. Its circumference is about 28km. The National Park is divided up into several protected zones, some of which may not be entered. In general it is forbidden to camp or to leave the signposted paths. It is only at the Playa de Taburiente that it is possible to camp for one night with permission from the park authorities (permission has to be obtained in advance from the Centro de Visitantes de El Paso).

Boat excursions

From Puerto de Tazacorte to Cueva Bonita and Playa de la Veta. Also boat trips from Santa Cruz.

Botanical gardens and Zoos

Culture Park »Pueblo Parque La Palma« (Los Llanos) with plants, animals, Canary houses and hand-made artefacts. »Maroparque« (Breña Alta) with plants and animals. Cactus Garden »Palmex« (Los Llanos). Bird Park »Parque Paraíso de las Aves« (El Paso).

Canyoning

There are demanding excursions for gorge climbers in the Barranco del Agua (at Los Tilos), in the Barranco Las Grajas (at Roque de los Muchachos) and in the Barranco de Fagundo (at El Tablado).

Caves

Up to now over 80 caves have been discovered, the longest of which is well over 1km long. The Cueva de Todoque is particularly spectacular. It is intended to open to tourists the 550m long pipes (Tubo) from lava stone, which can be walked through on the lava slopes of Volcano San Juan.

Climbing

La Palma only offers a couple climbing areas. The most well known is the Barranco de la Madera with routes from 4 – 7b+ and the Volcán Tajuya (at El Paso).

Diving

La Palma is an excellent diving area. Clubs are found in Santa Cruz, Los Cancajos, Puerto Naos, Puerto de Tazacorte.

Markets

Markets in the market halls of Santa Cruz and Los Llanos (daily 7–14.00). Farmers market in Mazo (Sat 15–20.00, Sun 8–13.00). On every first Sunday of the month there is a flea market, which alternates between Santa Cruz / Los Llanos.

Mountain biking and Cycling

The tracks on the Cumbres and the roads, which in places seldom see a lot of traffic, are excellent for cyclists and mountain bikers who are used to hills. Bike hire and guided tours for example in Los Cancajos, Los Llanos, Puerto Naos.

Museums

The Island Museum in Santa Cruz contains very interesting collections including paintings and prehistoric finds.

Paragliding

The island offers excellent opportunities for paragliding, especially on the lee side of Cumbre Vieja (Fuencaliente, Jedey) but also on the windward side (Santa Cruz). Clubs in Santa Cruz, Puerto Naos.

Picnic places

Picnic areas (Zona recreativa) equipped with barbeque facilities and playgrounds are popular destinations for the Palmeros.

Riding

There are some riding clubs (Breña Alta, El Paso), which also offer excursions.

Swimming

La Palma is not an exceptional bathing island but it does have some nice beaches – best known are Los Cancajos, Puerto Naos (Playa Nueva, Playa de los Monjas, Charco Verde), Fuencaliente (Playa Zamora, Playa Nueva) and Playa de Nogales near Puntallana, which is only suitable when the sea is calm. In the north there are no beaches for bathing (mainly rocky coast) but there are seawater swimming pools: Charco Azul (at San Andrés) and La Fajana (at Barlovento).

Information and Addresses

Getting there

La Palma is on the programme of some travel organisers and there are charter flights from most countries in Western Europe. Scheduled flights are only via Madrid. Moreover there are connecting flights to Tenerife, Gran Canaria, Lanzarote and El Hierro as well as ferries to Tenerife, La Gomera and El Hierro.

Information

Tourist offices: Patronato de Turismo, Avenida Maritima 3, E-38700 Santa Cruz de La Palma, Tel: 922 41 21 06, Fax: 922 42 00 30, www.la-palma-tur.org. Also tourist information in the airport and in the Oficina Insular del Turismo, Calle O'Daly 22, E-38700 Santa Cruz de La Palma, Tel: 922 41 19 57. *National Park:* Centro de Visitantes de El Paso (Visitor Centre) on the main road from El Paso – Santa Cruz (turning off in Cumbrecita) with exhibition and expert advise, Tel: 922 49 70 81, e-mail caldera@mma.es. Further National Park information centres in Cumbrecita and Pista Los Llanos – Barranco de las Angustias, at the Playa de Taburiente and on the summit car park at Roque de las Muchachos.

Accommodation

There are small campsites at Puntagorda and La Fajana (Barlovento), and it is possible to camp at some of the picnic sites (Zona recreativa / refugio; permission in the Forestry Office = Casa forestral) as well as on the Playa de Taburiente (permission from the National Park authorities). Unofficial camping is not permitted.

Climate

La Palma is dominated by a sub tropical climate with slight temperature variation between summer and winter. The weather is determined by the trade

Sunrise at Los Cancajos with the silhouette of the neighbouring island of Tenerife.

wind, a wind which brings wet, warm air masses from the northeast. This rises up the mountains and veils large parts of the island, particularly in the east, with a thick blanket of clouds.

CLIMATE TABLE FOR SANTA CRUZ DE LA PALMA													
Month		1	2	3	4	5	6	7	8	9	10	11	12	Year
Day	°C	21	21	22	22	22	24	25	26	26	26	24	22	23
Night	°C	15	14	15	16	17	18	19	21	21	19	18	16	17
Water	°C	19	18	19	19	19	20	22	23	22	22	21	20	20
Sunshine	hrs	5	6	6	7	8	9	10	9	8	6	5	5	7

Emergency phone numbers
General emergency phone number for fire service, police and emergency doctor: Tel. 112.

Festivals
The most well known is the Almond Festival, generally on the first Sunday in February in Puntagorda, the Carnival on Shrove Tuesday, Corpus Christi, the festival with a cattle market in San Antonio del Monte on the second weekend in June and of course the great island festival of the Bajada de la Virgen de las Nieves which takes place every five years.

Shop opening hours
Shops are generally open 9–13.00 (Mon–Sat) and 17–20.00 (Mon–Fri), banks 9–14.00 (Mon–Fri) Post offices 9–14.00 (Mon–Fri) / 9–12.00 (Sat).

Telephone
Dialling code for Spain: 0034

Theft
The crime rate is relatively low. Nevertheless one should not leave unattended valuables in cars or other places.

Transport
Buses: La Palma has a well-developed network of buses, especially between Santa Cruz and Los Llanos and on the east and west coasts, poor connections or none at all for the north and the Caldera high road. For these areas the use of a car or taxi is unavoidable.

Taxi: There is a taxi stand in most of the larger places – otherwise a taxi can be ordered from a bar. Taxi stands in Santa Cruz Tel: 922 41 12 02, Los Llanos Tel: 922 46 27 40, El Paso Tel: 922 48 50 03, Los Sauces Tel: 922 45 09 28.

Hire cars: Car hire is relatively cheap and cars can be hired in all of the larger towns and at the airport. In the high season it is best to book a car from one's home country. The roads on the island tend to be windy and minor roads are often very narrow, rough and steep. After rainfall there is a considerable risk of stone fall onto the roads and in the trade wind cloud zone there is often thick fog.

Observatories at Roque de los Muchachos.

1 **SANTA CRUZ DE LA PALMA** – **LOS LLANOS** (via Túnel gr.) (1'10")

Mo–Fr	6.15–20.15 every hour	6.30–20.30 every hour
Sa	6.15–13.15 every hr, 14.15–20.15 every 2 hrs	6.30–13.30 every hr, 14.30–20.30 every 2 hrs
Sun	6.15–20.15 every 2 hrs	6.30–20.30 every 2 hrs

2 **LOS LLANOS** – **PUERTO DE TAZACORTE** (20")
(via Tazacorte)

Mo–Sa	6.30–20.30 every hour	7.00–21.00 every hour
Sun	8.30–20.30 every hour	9.00–21.00 every hour

3 **SANTA CRUZ DE LA PALMA** – **LOS LLANOS** (1'25")
(via Mazo / Fuencaliente / Jedey) ■ = only to Fuencaliente, ● = only from Fuencaliente

Mo–Fr	8.00 / ■10.30 / 12.00 / ●12.15 / ■14.15 16.00 / ■18.15 / 20.15	6.00 / ●9.00 / 10.00 / ■11.30 / 14.00 / ■16.00 / ●17.00 / 18.00
Sa	8.00 / 12.00 / ●12.15 / 16.00 / 20.15	6.00 / 10.00 / ■11.30 / 14.00 / 18.00
Sun	12.00 / 20.15	10.00 / 18.00

4 **LOS LLANOS** – **PUERTO NAOS** (via La Laguna) (20")

Mo–Sa	6.30–20.30 every hr, 9.00–14.00 every 30 min	7.00–21.00 every hr, 9.30–14.30 every 30 min
Sun	8.30–20.30 every hour	9.00–21.00 every hour

5 **LOS LLANOS** – **GARAFÍA** (via Las Tricias) (2'00")

Mo–Sa	7.15 / 10.30 / 16.30 / 19.15	7.30 / 11.00 / 14.30 / 16.30
Sun	10.30 / 19.15	7.30 / 16.30

7 **SANTA CRUZ DE LA PALMA** – **TIGALATE** (Montes de Luna) (20")
(via Hoyo de Mazo / San Simón) ■ = only Mo–Fr

Mo–Sa	9.30 / 12.00 / ■14.15 / ■18.15	7.00 / 10.00 / ■12.30 / ■15.00 / 17.00

8 **SANTA CRUZ DE LA PALMA** – **AIRPORT** (via Los Cancajos) (15")

Mo–Fr	7.15–17.45 every 30 min / 18.45 / 19.45 / 20.45	8.15–18.15 every 30 min / 19.15 / 20.15 / 21.15
Sa–Sun	7.15 / 7.45–20.45 every hour	8.15 – 21.15 every hour

10 **SANTA CRUZ DE LA PALMA** – **BUENAVISTA** (via Las Nieves) (25")

Mo–Sa	7.45–11.45 every hr / 13.15 / 14.15 / 15.45 / 16.45 / 18.30 / 20.15 / 21.30	7.15–12.15 every hr / 13.45 / 15.15 / 16.15 / 17.15 / 19.30 / 20.45
Sun	8.45 / 10.45 / 13.15 / 15.45 / 18.30 / 20.15 / 21.30	8.15 / 9.15 / 12.15 / 15.15 / 16.15 / 19.30 / 20.45

11 **SANTA CRUZ DE LA PALMA** – **BARLOVENTO** (via Los Sauces) (1'20")
■ = on to / comes from Garafía (Arrival / Departure 90" later / earlier)

Mo–Fr	■7.10 / 8.10 / 10.10 / 12.10 / 14.10 / 16.10 / 18.10 / 20.10	6.30 / ■7.30 / 8.30 / 9.30 / 11.30 / 13.30 / ■15.30 / 17.30
Sa–Sun	8.10 / 10.10 / 14.10 / 18.10 / 20.10	■7.30 (only Sa) / 9.30 / 11.30 / 13.30 / 17.30

12 **LOS SAUCES** – **SAN ANDRÉS** (20")

daily	7.10 (Mo–Fr) / 9.10 / 11.10 / 14.10 / 17.10	7.30 (Mo–Fr) / 9.30 / 11.30 / 14.30 / 17.30

(Up-to-date bus timetables in the bus station or in »Info Magazin«)

Santa Cruz and the East

A treasure chest, lush cultivated land and laurel forest

Typical La Palma balcony on the Avenida Maritima in Santa Cruz.

Santa Cruz is not only the capital, but also the most beautiful and historical place on the island. A stroll through the leisurely but busy lanes of the old town should be on the programme for all visitors. For those with a car it is best to park in the city car park between the main traffic artery, the Avenida Maritima, and the sea. Bus passengers arrive directly at the Plaza de la Constitución (large square with traffic island on the south end of the Avenida Maritima), which lends itself as a starting point for a walk through the town. From there walk along the main shopping street, Calle O'Daly (pedestrian zone) with its splendid town houses (particularly fine is the Palacio Salazar with the Tourist Office) to the Plaza d'España, the gem of the old town. The romantic triangular plaza is lined by the Iglesia del Salvador, the magnificent town hall and some splendid town houses. At the end of the Calle O'Daly turn left into the Avenida del Puente and so arrive at the Teatro Chico and the Market Hall at the Plaza de Mercado. On the right next to the Market Hall continue to the Placeta de Borrero and straight on to the shady Plaza de la Alameda. In the middle of the square is a smart kiosk; at the end the museum ship »Santa Maria« a replica of Columbus' ship. Keep right to reach the coastal road Avenida Maritima, along which it is possible to admire the typical balconies of the Canaries. This leads back to the starting point. Another »must see« is the Church of Las Nieves and the Mirador de la Concepción with its fine views.

The southeast of the island can be called the Garden of La Palma. This is not only the traditional agricultural area of the island but also the villa suburbs of Santa Cruz, *Breña Baja* and *Breña Alta* are found here. Numerous palm groves including dragon trees are also part of the landscape. The tourist stronghold of the east, *Los Cancajos*, also belongs to the parish of Breña Baja. Around the promenade and the beautiful black sands there is a cluster of hotels and apartment blocks. A bit further south is the airport and higher up the area of *Mazo* (El Pueblo) is joined on. The Mercadillo, which takes place every Saturday and Sunday, is of interest as is the Cueva de Belmaco (Parque arqueológico de Belmaco; Mon–Sat 10–18.00, Sun 10–14.00) in which the first cave engravings done by the original inhabitants were discovered 250 years ago. A little to the north of the caves unsurfacced roads branch off from the main road to the beach communities at the Playa del Pozo, the Playa del Burro and the Playa las Salineras.

Leaving the island capital on the coast road to the north, *Puntallana* is reached, which with the Playa de Nogales has the only beach in the northeast. The beautiful sandy beach of about 250 metres in length is best reached from El Granel, the last part has to be covered on foot. Deep green gorges, terraced fields and steep mountain slopes now dominate the landscape. Further to the north *La Galga* is passed with the Miradores of San Bartolomé and La Montaña. The laurel forest of La Galga is also worthy of attention: along with Los Tilos it is one of the original rainforests of the island. Shortly before Los Sauces it is worth making a detour to *San Andrés*, one of the most beautiful villages on the island. The neat and dainty lanes and squares of the town, which is surrounded by banana plantations, invites one to spend some time here. To the north is the seawater swimming pool of Charco Azul. A few kilometres after the turning off to San Andrés the branch road to *Los Tilos* turns off: the area around the Barranco del Agua offers numerous excellent walks. Further on along the coastal road the main town of the northeast, *Los Sauces* is reached. With its splendid Plaza and the large church this town almost has the appearance of a city.

LOS TILES BIOSPHERE PROTECTION AREA

The almost undisturbed laurel forest with its lush sub-tropical flora has been declared a biosphere protection area by UNESCO and is one of the most famous natural wonders of the island. The protected area, which was increased to 13,420 ha in 1988, extends from Puntallana in the south to Gallegos in the north-west and joins the Caldera de Taburiente National Park in the west. At the entrance to the core area of the reserve is found Los Tilos, 500m, Visitor Centre (open daily 8.30–17.00) and a restaurant (3km from the road Santa Cruz–Los Sauces; turning off from the road 1km before Los Sauces; bus number 11 stops here).

1 From Santa Cruz to Las Nieves, 260m

From the Museum ship to the Church of the Island Saints

Santa Cruz – Barranco del Río de Las Nieves – Las Nieves – Barranco de la Madera – Santa Cruz

Starting point: Museum ship »Santa Maria« in the Plaza de la Alameda / Avenida de las Nieves in Santa Cruz de La Palma (bus stop for buses 1, 3, 6-11, 14) on the northern edge of the town.

Walking time: Ascent 1 hr, return route ¾ hr; total time 1¾ hr.
Ascent: 250m.
Grade: Easy road and valley walk.
Refreshment: In Santa Cruz and the Bar-Restaurant Parrilla in the Plaza near the Church of Las Nieves.
Alternative: From Las Nieves to the Mirador de la Concepción: From the church go down the road in a westerly direction as far as the bridge over the Barranco del Río de las Nieves. 20m after the bridge there is a steep, wide paved path, which goes off right and leads in hairpins up to Velhoco (¼ hr). Now go straight on along the busy tarmac road, finally crossing the Carretera de Timibucar to the Mirador de la Concepcíon (¾ hr; →Walk 2).

The pilgrimage church of Nuestra Señora de Las Nieves is dedicated to the protective guardian of the island, the Virgin of the Snows and is among the finest churches on La Palma. Every five years the Bajada de la Virgen de las Nieves is celebrated, the biggest and most well known festival on the island, the high point of which is the procession of the figure of Mary to the Museum ship, the Santa Maria. This walk also takes in the route of the pilgrimage.

From the **Plaza de la Alameda** go along the road up the Barranco. After a few minutes it crosses to the other side of the barranco and continues uphill along its right-hand edge. A few minutes after the

The path just before Las Nieves.

bridge – the last houses of a large housing estate have been left behind – a cemented track forks off left from the road into the Barranco del Río de Las Nieves which is followed (straight on is the Barranco de la Madera, the return route for later). Shortly after the turning off, a tunnel can be seen on the left, which leads to the main road from Santa Cruz, the Avenida del Puente. However, continue straight on for a stretch until a gravelled path turns off left through the generally dry streambed. After a stable this becomes a camino which switches to the right bank after a few minutes, goes between two stone walls for a short time, later twice switches river bank and finally turns into a track which leads to the Velhoco – Las Nieves road. A good 100m before the junction with the road a camino forks off right, along which the **Plaza de las Nieves,** with the pilgrimage church of the same name, can be reached directly.

For the return route, go down some steps on the left of the Bar-Restaurant Parrilla in the church square to the road, which immediately after crossing the Barranco de la Madera, is left for an unsurfaced road which branches off to the right. This follows the edge of the Barranco and and turns into a proper road which (soon on the familiar route) leads back to **Santa Cruz.**

2 From Santa Cruz to the Mirador de la Concepción, 355m

To one of the outstanding viewpoints of the island

Santa Cruz (Mercado) – Mirador de la Concepción and back

Starting point: Market Hall (Mercado) on the Avenida del Puente, the main street of Santa Cruz de La Palma (bus stop for buses 1, 3, 6-11, 14).
Walking time: Santa Cruz – Mirador de la Concepción 1½ hrs, return route 1 hr; total time 2½ hrs.
Ascent: Nearly 350m.
Grade: Steep road walk but mainly away from the main road.
Refreshment: In Santa Cruz and at the crossroads by the Mirador.
Combination possible with Walk 1 (see there).

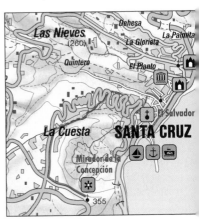

Chapel at Mirador de la Concepción.

The Mirador de la Concepción is the most impressive viewpoint over Santa Cruz de La Palma – an absolute must for every visitor to the island and for every keen photographer. Of course, this mirador with its pretty chapel can be reached by car or bus, but the ascent via the suggested path is a much finer and more interesting way to reach the mirador. The route largely follows peaceful caminos and minor roads through what were once very early suburbs of Santa Cruz.

From the **Market hall** go for a short 5 minutes up along the main street (Avenida del Puente), until on the

View down to Santa Cruz from Mirador de la Concepción.

left by a kiosk steps branch off which lead up a cultivated hillside. One level higher continue straight on up the hill until the camino/road leads into the *Carretera de Timibucar*, the connecting road between Santa Cruz and the Mirador de la Concepcíon, which leads uphill in numerous hairpins. Go for a short distance along this little used country road until on the right a steep road forks off in a straight line thereby cutting off the broad hairpins of the country road. It leads through the middle of a residential area, which is spread out over the complete ridge of land. The country road is crossed several times and the view back to the capital city of the island becomes more and more impressive.

After a good hour – the last part of the ascent is particularly strenuous – the worst is over: a high plateau is reached (a former monastery is on the left) and it is only necessary to follow the country road to the left and then to take the first road turning off on the left at a bar which leads to the **Mirador de la Concepción** (20 minutes along the road).

Next to the circular flowerbed is a pretty chapel: whitewashed and with in-set lava stone. It has a delicate balcony and is crowned with a tiny bell tower.

3 From Mazo to Monte Breña, 565m

Along quiet roads and tracks to a viewpoint above the airport

Mazo – El Molino – Monte Breña – Mazo

Starting point: Market hall in Mazo (El Pueblo), 430m (bus stop for bus 3), in the side street above the church.
Walking time: Mazo – Monte Breña good 1½ hrs, Monte Breña – Mazo 1¼ hrs; total time 2¾ hrs.
Ascent: Good 300m.
Grade: Easy walking along tracks and little-used roads.
Refreshment: In bars and restaurants in Mazo.
Combination possible with walk 4.

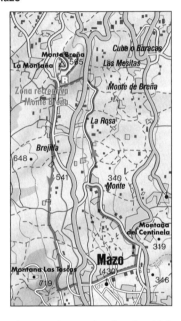

Monte Breña with its altitude of only 565m does not belong to the showpiece summits of the island. Nevertheless, this very prominent viewpoint above Breña Baja, which is accessible via a road, is worth an excursion.

The walk begins at the Market hall in **Mazo**, so it is possible to take advantage of this and include a visit to the Mercadillo: every Saturday (15-20.00) and Sunday (8-13.00) local products are offered for sale. Go down the steep Calle General Mola, past a cemetery and a church, which are also worth a visit, and follow the steep little road that leads off to the left from the church. In a bend, go straight on along the minor road (Camino El Llanito), which splits shortly afterwards. Here go right (Sign: »El Molino«) until the road splits; now go left and left again, which brings one to the old **mill**, in which nowadays a pottery and shop are situated.

Continue along the road past the mill and go rightwards through a portal decorated with a cross and continue to the left down along a concreted track, which immediately leads to a road. Now walk up the road (after a few minutes a gallery on the left) until after about 20 minutes in a sharp left-hand bend a road (Camino El Linar) forks off to the right. Keep going straight on along this, directly towards Monte Breña, which faces one with its broad scree flank. After a total of 1¼ hrs the main road from Breña Alta/Baja to

Garden landscape at the foot of Monte Breña.

Mazo is reached at the foot of Monte Breña. This is crossed, and immediately opposite the road is followed which rises to the left at the foot of the mountain. At a canal it becomes a footpath and leads up to the **Montaña la Breña picnic area** with tables, benches and barbecue places. From here either go up directly over the scree slope, or, nicer and more leisurely, go right in a wide curve up along the pine covered hill to the viewing platform on the summit of **Monte Breña**. The panoramic view extends from the Cumbres to the east coast between Santa Cruz and Mazo.

Now go back to the picnic place, and from there continue along the road towards the south. In the left-hand bend after a good 10 minutes turn off straight on along the tarmac road. This almost immediately becomes a track, which is now followed straight on. After 5 minutes it goes up more steeply to the next small rise, which is, however, left to the left, passing a farmhouse. The track finally ends in a partly asphalted gravelled road (here the Camino de la Faya, →Walk 4, crosses it), which is also followed straight on. At the first houses in Mazo the walk follows a road for 100m, which it leaves down to the left. Here continue straight on along the track (Camino las Toscas). After a good 5 minutes, 50m after a picnic place (possible ascent to the Montaña Las Toscas, 719m), turn left in the dip in the road onto a paved path, which crosses a road half way along, and leads down to the nearby main street in **Mazo** (bus stop). Opposite, the steep paved street – Calle General Mola – leads in a few minutes to the Mercadillo.

5 From Breña Alta to San Isidro

Canal walk along the quiet woods at the foot of the Cumbre Nueva

San Pedro de Breña Alta – Carretera de la Cumbre – Canal de Fuenca-liente – San Isidro – San Pedro de Breña Alta

Starting point: Plaza of San Pedro de Breña Alta, 344m (bus stop for buses 1, 6, 14).

Walking time: San Pedro – start of canal path nearly 1 hr, Canal path 2½ hrs, end of canal path – San Pedro 1 hr; total time 4½ hrs.

Ascent: 450m.

Grade: Apart from a short airy section along the canal, generally straightforward but slightly strenuous walking.

Refreshment: Bars and restaurants in San Pedro.

Alternative: Short circular route via the Canal de Laja Breña (1¾ hrs in total; beautiful view over Breña Alta and Breña Baja): After the arched bridge (20 min from San Pedro) a track goes off left which leads up to the Canal de Laja Breña. Follow this in a southerly direction, crossing another bridge with arches and past dog kennels. After 20 minutes the canal leads

The Canal de Laja Breña.

between houses and crosses a cemented road. A good 20 minutes later before a valley the canal crosses another cemented road. Here leave the canal and walk leftwards down the car track. This ends after 15 minutes in the Barranco del Llanito in a road which leads immediately to the left into the main road to San Pedro. Now carry on left as described below.

Combination possible with Walks 6 and 29.

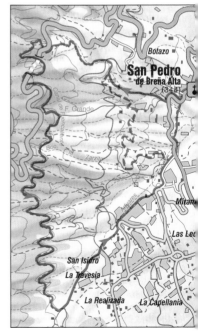

The smart town of San Pedro de Breña Alta.

This walk through the thickly forested slopes at the foot of the Cumbre Nueva is suitable for any time of the year, especially for not so nice days. In autumn the splendid colours of the chestnut trees are fascinating and in the winter half of the year passionate fungi hunters can collect chanterelles and other mushrooms.

From the plaza in **San Pedro de Breña Alta** follow the main road to the south (Mazo direction). 5 minutes later, immediately after crossing the Barranco de Laja, leave the main road and turn right onto the road, which leads down into the bottom of the barranco. After a quarter of an hour keep right at the fork and go under the arched bridge over the *Canal de Laja Breña* (→Alternative). Shortly after this the road becomes a narrow path, which goes directly upwards along the bed of the barranco. After a few minutes it crosses a covered canal. A good 5 minutes later it turns to the right towards the hillside and after a short incline ends in a camino at right angles to it. Follow this to the left. It crosses the base of the valley and climbs – at the fork after 100m left again – up the slope past a stone house. Shortly after this the camino crosses a track (15m to the left) and a good 10 minutes later it meets the main road (*Carretera de la Cumbre*). Follow this up for about 50m until the old camino continues on the right. This goes up steeply at first over steps and after a good 5 minutes, crosses a covered canal (*Canal de Fuencaliente*), which now provides the line of the walk. (If the canal has been overlooked, shortly after the camino passes a stone bench, thus indicating that one has gone too far).

Ascent through the Barranco de Laja.

So now follow the canal to the left. After a good 10 minutes it goes above and past the Túnel Chico; shortly after a track crosses the canal. Stay along the canal, which in places is narrow and airy, and is moreover exposed to the danger of stone fall in strong wind and rain. It goes directly over the main road (one can also follow the parallel track!). After nearly 10 minutes the canal crosses the main road. Follow the road for about 50m to the next bend and go down to the left before the bridge to the canal along which the barranco is crossed (somewhat exposed!). The canal now mainly goes along through beautiful chestnut and rain forest; here and there tracks cross over the path. After three quarters of an hour cross a barranco with a large pipe. Half an hour later, cross a bridge over a bramble-filled barranco. Nearly 10 minutes later at the next mountain ridge another track crosses the canal – from here there is a fine view of Breña Baja and towards San Isidro. Immediately afterwards in the next small valley pass a house right next to the canal (bridge). Within the next 35 minutes three further barrancos are crossed (after 10 minutes a small barranco bridge, 10 minutes later next barranco, 15 minutes later another barranco bridge). Afterwards the canal track, which is rather overgrown for a while, swings right into a wide valley, which leads the canal over a long viaduct (left on the other side of the valley is a round reservoir). Here it is recommended to climb down left, more or less without a path to a track, and to then to go back up right to the canal along the track in the base of the valley – a few metres before the canal bridge the canal can be regained by going up a path on the left; after 50m this crosses a minor road on the other side of the valley. (The road can also be reached by following the track in the base of the valley to the left.)

Leave the canal now and follow the minor road down to the left (possibility to climb up to the Refugio El Pilar on the right, →Walk 6). It goes past the large reservoir and allows fine views towards Breña Alta. After a quarter of an hour the minor road joins a road, which is followed straight on downwards. It becomes narrower after 100m and after a good 5 minutes in the area of **San Isidro**, 570m, in a hairpin bend it touches on the main road to the Refugio El Pilar. Stay on the village road, which goes straight on downwards and which 10 minutes later meets the main road at a further hairpin bend (Km 1). Straight on is a cemented road, which splits after 100m. Here stay left and after 10 minutes reach the main road to San Pedro in the Barranco del Llanito. Follow this leftwards over a bridge and 50m later take the road which bears downwards to the right. This goes directly towards San Pedro and ends after 10 minutes in the Barranco de Laja in a road from which 25m further up a cemented road goes off right. This goes steeply up for a short distance and then forks – here go on left past a cross and then left up the Calle El Correo to the main street, which leads back right to the Plaza of **San Pedro de Breña Alta**.

Viaduct on the Canal de Fuencaliente at the end of the canal walk.

6 From Breña Alta to El Paso

Crossing from east to west

San Pedro de Breña Alta – San Isidro – Pared Vieja – Refugio El Pilar – Centro de Visitantes de El Paso

Starting point: Plaza of San Pedro de Breña Alta, 344m (bus stop for buses 1, 6, 14).
Destination: Centro de Visitantes de El Paso, 870m (bus stop for bus 1) at the upper end of El Paso.
Walking time: San Pedro – San Isidro 1 hr, San Isidro – Pared Vieja 1½ hrs, Pared Vieja – Refugio El Pilar ¾ hr, Refugio El Pilar – Centro de Visitantes 1¾ hrs; total time 5 hrs.

Ascent: 1150m plus a good 600m of descent.
Grade: Long, generally easy walk, which requires a sense of direction.
Refreshment: Bar-restaurants in San Pedro and El Paso.
Combination possible with Walks 5, 30 and 32.

The Camino real from Breña Alta to El Paso over the Cumbre Vieja is the oldest connecting route between the east coast and the Aridane Valley. This is also the reason for the misleading names of Cumbre Nueva (»young Cumbre«) and the geologically much younger Cumbre Vieja (»old Cumbre«).

From the Plaza in **San Pedro** follow the main road to the south (direction of Mazo) and turn left into the first street (Calle El Correo) to continue right onto the narrow village road after a few metres. At the fork after 50m (cross) stay right again and so reach a road down in the base of the Barranco de Laja. Follow this for 25m to the left and then turn right onto a minor road, which leads in a leisurely fashion up the other side of the valley and after about 15 minutes of walking in total joins the main road to Mazo. After only 100m, just after the bridge, leave the main road for a road which goes off to the right (Camino la Union), which immediately forks. Keep right here and follow the road up through the Barranco Norza. After a few minutes this becomes a gravel road and soon leads under two bridges next to a culvert. Soon after go under two further aqueducts in short succession. About 100m further on (20 min from the main road) an old camino cuts across the track. This is then followed to the left. The narrow somewhat overgrown pathed path leads up to a rock wall and after 5 minutes a high meadow area is reached, along which is a track. This is followed to the right and at the fork shortly after go straight on (not right). The track now crosses a

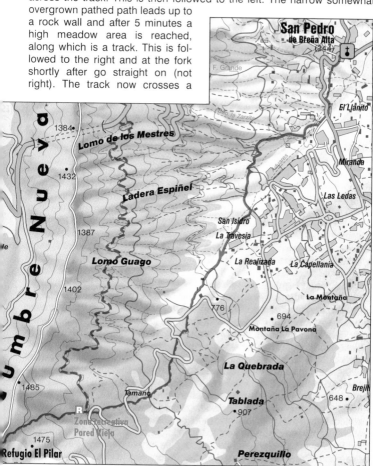

7 Cubo de La Galga

Easy valley walk in the Biosphere Reserve of Los Tiles

La Galga – Cubo de La Galga and back

Location: La Galga, 390m (bus stop for bus 11), 19km to the north of Santa Cruz on the main road to Barlovento.

Starting point: Go nearly 1km northwards along the main road from La Galga as far as the road tunnel. Immediately before the tunnel and 75m along the gravel road there is a good place to park.

Walking time: 1¾ hrs.

Ascent: 250m.

Grade: Easy valley walk.

Alternative: Sure-footed walkers who have a head for heights can add on a very worthwhile circuit through the cliffs above the gorge (good ½ hr): Through the gate under the canal continue up the valley along the fern-covered path, which splits after about 25m. Here keep left (the camino which goes straight on through the Barranco de la Galga and is partly paved, is soon more heavily overgrown) and follow the obvious path up the hillside. After a good 10 minutes, the path gets flatter, and leads across the hillside accompanied by a large water pipe, reached after a good 5 minutes. On the right (after 100m of road) it is possible in ½ hour to descend to La Galga. To the left the narrow airy canal path can be reached, along which it takes a good 10 minutes to get back to Cubo de la Galga – half way along there is a rocky promontory with splendid views over the barranco.

This walk leads to a beautiful gorge dominated by a splendid rain forest, which is part of the protected biosphere area of Los Tiles.

Immediately before the **tunnel** a gravel road goes off left leading easily upwards into the twisting gorge of the Barranco de la Galga. Almost immediately the scenery becomes more varied: the valley narrows appreciably, wild creepers hang down from the rock walls and the trees, ferns and laurels replace the bramble hedges. After about 25 minutes an aqueduct spans the path. A quarter of an hour later the track splits. A wide track goes off sharply to the left to Cubo de la Galga, to which a detour is made on the return route. However, continue straight on along the track to reach another fork after a few more minutes – straight on again (the left fork through the turnstile ends after a few minutes at two concrete barracks and a tunnel). The track ends shortly after in a light-filled valley basin at a massive, partly overhanging rock wall, which is intersected by a barranco and over which there is a waterfall after it has rained. The small, if not completely perfect paradise (iron girders and remains of walls do not quite fit the picture) is perfect for a rest.

The end of the first section of the walk is a beautiful rock basin.

Afterwards go back to the fork in the track, which leads to the Cubo de la Galga. The track becomes a path after 50m. Keep to the left at the fork a few minutes later (the path which goes straight on ends almost immediately at a small rock step, next to a spoil heap: the **Cubo de la Galga**) and so reach a canal and a valley basin. A path, along which one can explore the Barranco de la Galga (→Alternative), continues through the gate under the canal. Go back, however, along the road to the starting point.

8 To the Marcos and Cordero Springs

Adventurous tunnel-canal walk above the Barranco del Agua

Casa del Monte – Nacientes Marcos y Cordero and back

Location: Verada de las Lomadas, 240m (bus stop for number 11 bus), 3km from Los Sauces on the main road from Santa Cruz – Barlovento.
Starting point: Casa del Monte, 1330m. Approach from Verada de las Lomadas: in the left-hand bend at the entrance to the village in the direction of Los Sauces a steep, well signposted concrete road forks to the left (sign: »Casa del Monte / Nacientes Marcos y Cordero« – watch out! The left turn is still in the village: do not go up the extremely steep concrete road!) After 2km the road becomes a pista along which 10km later the stone house of Casa del Monte at the canal is reached – very bumpy in parts).

Walking time: Casa del Monte – Marcos Springs 1¼ hrs, Marcos Springs – Cordero Spring 20 min, return route 1½ hrs; total time 3 hrs (from Verada de las Lomadas an extra 5–6 hrs; signposted walking route away from the track).
Ascent: About 150m from Case del Monte (from Verada de las Lomadas an extra 1100m).
Grade: Easy, but frequently rather airy walking along a canal (sure-footedness and a head for heights needed). A powerful torch and a waterproof are necessary for the tunnel sections (some pitch dark, one section is more than 200m long!).
Combination possible with Walks 9 and 10 (ascent/descent from Los Tilos).

The walk along the canal to the Marcos and Cordero springs is an adventure in itself: the route runs high up in the steep walls above the Barranco del Agua, and there are no fewer than 13 tunnels. A good torch is a requirement for the rock passages, which in places are very narrow and low (it is frequently necessary to walk stooped and to watch out for projections on the roof). Moreover a waterproof is also necessary.

The approach drive from Las Lomadas to Casa del Monte can be problematic: the first few kilometres are mainly ok for driving, but after that the surface is bumpier. It is best to drive as far as possible and to do the last section up to the Casa del Monte on foot (en route there is also a footpath which branches off to the Casa del Monte).

At the **Casa del Monte** go left towards the canal. After just 10 minutes the first tunnel is reached, the entrance to which has an open barred door. 5 minutes later is the next, shorter tunnel and after 25 minutes the longest (over 200m). After a further half an hour – by which time 6 tunnels have been traversed – the basin is reached with a view of the Marcos Springs. Here continue on over the wall next to the basin. Go through another 2 tunnels, after which it is necessary to move quickly to avoid getting wet: in the last (12th) tunnel before the Marcos Springs there are a number of showers and torrents. The numerous cascades of the **Marcos Springs** present a fantastic natural spectacle – they are the most important springs outside the Caldera.

Now there is a short steeper uphill section of path, which for a while is away from the canal. The steep section is quickly overcome, there is another tunnel and the no less impressive cascades of the **Cordero Spring** are reached. Here the path ends. On the right it is possible to descend through the Barranco del Agua to Los Tilos (→Walk 10).

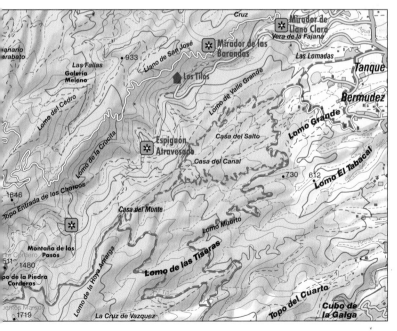

9 From Los Tilos to Casa del Monte, 1320m

Along a steep track for canal workers through the magic laurel forest

Los Tilos – Espigón Atravesado – Casa del Monte and back

Location: Los Sauces, 266m (bus stop for buses 11 and 12).
Starting point: Los Tilos, 500m, or the beginning of the forestry track about 500m from Los Tilos.
Walking time: Los Tilos – Espigón Atravesada 1 hr, Espigón Atravesado – Casa del Monte 1½ hrs, Return route just 2 hrs; total time 4½ hrs.
Ascent: About 850m.
Grade: Often very narrow, extremely steep and sloping path, which demands absolute sure-footedness and a head for heights (short easy climbing section). If the weather is unsettled (rain or strong wind) this walk should absolutely be avoided.
Refreshment: Bar-Restaurant in Los Tilos.
Alternative: From the Casa del Monte it is possible to descend to Verada de las

Lomadas (2¼ hrs).
Combination possible with Walks 8 (torch and waterproof!), 10 and 11.

The Canal Workers' Track from Los Tilos to Casa del Monte offers the ambitious mountain walker the opportunity to take in the Marcos and Cordero Springs in a large-scale circuit (→Walks 8, 10).

500 metres before **Los Tilos** a forestry road forks off up the hill (sign: »Monte el Canal y Los Tilos«). After a few minutes it goes through a 100m long tunnel and leads high over the base of the Barranco del Agua, to which, by the way, after 15 minutes a walk leads down (an interesting detour: after the descent along the narrow, slippery steps it is necessary to cross an exposed canal bridge and finally to climb down a 3m high rock step; →Walk 12). A good 5 minutes later an irrigation channel is passed on the left of the forestry track. About 30m later an obvious path branches off to the left, which has steps in places and leads up leftwards through the laurel forest. At the fork after a quarter of an hour keep right. The path now leads impressively across the steep slope, roughly staying at the same height. In parts it is rather narrow and sloping and in some places it is also somewhat exposed. After a quarter of an hour a short narrow mountain ridge is reached. The route now goes clearly upwards again and splits after 5 minutes.

There are only occasional views towards the Barranco del Agua and the Cumbre.

Straight on is an extremely steep climb to Casa del Canal – here bear right down over steps to the forestry track 25m away. Here it is worthwhile after 10m to take a path on the right with steps as a detour to the **Espigón Atravesado**, 754m (5 minutes).

Continue along the forestry track up the valley. After a good 10 minutes a path goes off right to the Cordero Spring (→Walk 10). 10 minutes later the forestry track ends at a cable railway for materials. 50m before the end of the track an obvious, partially stepped path goes off to the left. It serves the canal workers for access to the canals in the cliff and winds its way – apart from a short traverse after 10 minutes – very steeply and directly up through the wonderful laurel forest. After just a quarter of an hour a covered up canal is reached. Follow this to the right with a fantastic view over the Barranco del Agua and a little waterfall on the left in the rock wall. After only a few minutes a path forks off up to the left parallel to the canal, again very steep, in places also exposed (easy climbing sections). After about 5 minutes the path leads leftwards across the hillside – now not so steep – to reach the level of the ridge (good 15 min). This is reached directly at the **Casa del Monte** (connection to →Walk 8).

10 From Los Tilos to the Cordero Spring

Through the rainforest to the source of the Palmeros' wealth

Los Tilos – Barranco del Agua – Naciente Cordero and back

Location: Los Sauces, 266m (bus stop for buses 11 and 12).
Starting point: Los Tilos, 500m, or the beginning of the forestry track, approximately 500m before it.
Walking time: Los Tilos – 1st bridge 1¼ hrs, 1st bridge – 2nd bridge 1½ hrs, 2nd bridge – Cordero 1 hr, descent 3 hrs; total time 6¾ hrs.
Ascent: About 900m.
Grade: Long strenuous walk, from 1st bridge via a camino, short sections possibly narrow and affected by landslip, from 2nd bridge almost without a path in a mainly dry streambed (danger of stonefall!). Hardly any problems with navigation, but sure-footedness and a head for heights necessary. The path should not be walked after heavy rainfall.
Refreshment: Bar-Restaurant in Los Tilos.
Alternative: Experienced, fit mountaineers, who are absolutely sure-footed and unaffected by vertigo (a number of protected sections, often very steep and exposed, and possibly overgrown) can also return to Los Tilos via the Sendero de Pasos de Cordero and the Mirador de las Barandas: the obvious path forks off after about 5 min below the Cordero Spring to the left of the return path (cairns). Immediately go steeply left at the junction and at a further junction after 20 min to the right uphill across the hillside. A few minutes later the narrow climb leads through a side barranco (protection by a chain) and continues up and down across the steep slope above the Barranco del Agua. After a total of an hour a small mountain ridge, which leads to the valley, is reached (fork). Here go up left over the ridge to a small stone wall (good 10 min), in front of which it is necessary to go to the right for a bit

and then up very steep steps to a further ridge (good 10 min; sign: »Sendero de Pasos de Cordero«). A few minutes later the path across the slope joins a forestry track (1½ hrs from Cordero). Down right along this for 15 min as far as a fork (white dots as markings) continuing as for Walk 46 to the Mirador de las Barandas. From here via Walk 13 to Los Tilos (4 hrs from Cordero Spring; the most difficult walk in this guide!).
Combination possible with walks 8 and 9 (Cordero – Casa del Monte – Los Tilos).

The beautiful path up to the Cordero Spring.

The day's walk from Los Tilos to the Cordero Spring leads deep into the gorges and laurel wood wilderness of the north east – mainly through the landslide endangered slopes above the Barranco del Agua, and finally in an adventurous fashion along the base of the Barranco.

From **Los Tilos** go back about 500m along the tarmac road to the right fork of the forestry road Monte El Canal and Los Tilos (sign, parking on the road) which is now followed. The road goes through a tunnel, passes a stone house and after just an hour reaches the first big fork (a path leads sharply to the left in 5 min to the **Espigón Atravesado** of Walk 11). However, stay on the forestry road, until after about 10 minutes steps go off right (sign: »Sendero de Marcos y Cordero«), which lead down to a **wooden bridge** which can already be seen from above. On the other side the path leads up in a leisurely fashion and continues steadily now leftwards soon high above the Barranco del Agua. Here and there, in the crossing of steep slopes and (mainly dry) tributary streams one has to expect narrow sections and even some parts which have slightly collapsed or have been buried. However this is generally not a problem for sure-footed mountain walkers. Gradually mighty pines also now appear in the thinning laurel forest, which up to now provided a reliable source of shade. Broom, rock roses and numerous other forms of flowering vegetation are also to be found. After a total of 2½ hrs

The last section of the walk leads directly through the Barranco del Agua.

Numerous cascades fall into the canal at the neighbouring Marcos Springs.

there is a view of the light again: a lookout point protected by railings awaits us with a beautiful view down into the deeply gouged-out green-covered barranco.

A few minutes later there is a fork to the left, but stay to the right on the path with steps, which soon switches valley sides via a **wooden bridge**. Immediately after the bridge, go down into the streambed and go up along here for about a quarter of an hour (not up the path on the right, which is very steep and slippery!). The following rock step in the barranco is avoided on the right by a path marked with cairns (the turning off, which is 50m before the rock step, is marked by a horizontal red line on a boulder in the stream bed). After a few minutes the path leads back into the bed of the barranco, which is mainly dry – a difficult but nevertheless incredibly beautiful ascent. Finally the end of the valley comes into sight and the distance noise of water draws nearer. Tree trunks across the path, boulders and a thicket provide something of an obstacle but cairns, finally keeping to the left, indicate the best route. Then the **Cordero Spring** is reached: an idyllic spot surrounded by superabundant displays of flowers. At this point a number of springs shoot out of the wall before our eyes and pour their valuable liquid into the canal, which also takes in the Marcos Springs en route and provides the whole region of San Andrés and Sauces with water.

11 Monte El Canal y Los Tilos

A stroll through the UNESCO Biosphere Reserve

Los Tilos – Pista Monte El Canal y Los Tilos – Mirador and back

Location: Los Sauces, 266m (bus stop for buses 11 and 12).
Starting point: Los Tilos, 500m, or the beginning of the forestry road »Pista Monte El Canal y Los Tilos«, about 500m before Los Tilos.
Walking time: Los Tilos – Mirador 1 hr, Return route ¾ hr; total time 1¾ hrs.
Ascent: About 300m.
Grade: Easy, leisurely walk through a wood on forestry roads.
Refreshment: Bar-Restaurant Los Tilos.
Alternative: Return route from Espigón Atravesado (for sure-footed mountain walkers with a head for heights): 10m after the turn off for Espigón Atravesado a path

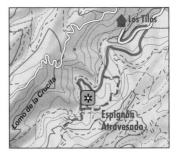

goes off to the left from the forestry road. There is a short section up steps and then it splits after 25m. Here continue left. The narrow path first goes down slightly to the left and then on the level across the steep hillside to fork again after 20 min. Here bear left along an obvious path descending in 10 min to the forestry road, which leads back rightwards to the starting point in a good 15 min.
Combination possible with Walks 9, 10.

A walk along the Forestry road Monte El Canal y Los Tilos is an absolute must for every walker, but particularly so for the nature lover who is interested in botany. The Laurel jungle, which was declared a Biosphere Reserve by UNESCO in 1983, is situated in one of the rainiest regions of the island and offers a particular lush flora, which is characterised by giant ferns and numerous liana-like climbing plants, which hang down from the rock walls and the trees. At the end of the walk a beautiful viewpoint awaits,

Rest at the Espigón Atravesado.

View over the Barranco del Agua with the Mirador Espigón Atravesado in the centre of the picture.

which provides a magnificent overview of the gorge wilderness of the Barranco del Agua.

The actual path begins 500m before **Los Tilos**. Here a forestry road, which is closed to cars, branches off up the hill (sign: »Monte El Canal y Los Tilos«). After a few minutes this leads through a 100m long tunnel and then one is in the middle of the paradise-like rain forest. To the right, down below, water rushes through canals in the Barranco del Agua, down into which, after a quarter of an hour, a narrow, slippery staircase leads. Stay on the forestry road however. There are few places where any light penetrates through the dense laurel forest, which has covered even the steepest rock walls, with climbing plants hanging down towards the road. A good 5 minutes later an irrigation channel is passed and shortly after a stone house. The gravel track leads up a bit more steeply now, until after three quarters of an hour a wide junction is reached (turning place). Here a narrow path with steps goes off sharply to the left and leads in 5 minutes along a mountain ridge, in places protected by a railing, to a beautiful viewpoint, 754m (**Espigón Atravesado**, measuring station). The little path, which forks off left at the junction after 10m, is a wonderful alternative for the return route (→Alternative). Keen botanists should follow the forestry road to the end at a cable car for materials (20 min; possible ascent to the Casa del Monte, →Walk 9).

12 Barranco del Agua

Short, but impressive gorge adventure

Los Tilos – Barranco del Agua and back

Location: Los Sauces, 266m (bus stop for buses 11 and 12).
Starting point: Los Tilos, 500m.
Walking time: 1 hr there and back.
Ascent: Insignificant.
Grade: Easy walk – nevertheless no path in the streambed, so sure-footedness an advantage. Only for good weather conditions (danger of stone fall!)
Refreshment: Bar-Restaurant Los Tilos.

Really this walk is more of a short excursion than a real walk. Nevertheless, it provides as good an impression of the wilderness and luxuriant, rain forest flora of the north east side of the island as any other walk. When raining or after heavy rainfall one should avoid this short walk – not only on account of the rising water in the gorge which is only 2 metres wide in places, but especially because of the stone fall which should not be underestimated below the overhanging fern and creeper covered rock walls.

From **Los Tilos** go back for a few metres along the tarmac road, until shortly before the **bridge** over the Agua stream. Here a path goes off to the right, which follows a canal for a few metres and then leads down into the streambed. Now it continues upstream, continually switching banks. Half way along – the first overhanging rock wall has already been passed – a narrowing in the gorge is reached, which is only a few metres wide. Water sprays down here from a canal. A further extremely overhanging rock wall follows (leave the stone fall endangered spot as fast as possible) to arrive shortly after at a rock step, which is overcome with the help of a ladder. (A few metres before the rock step it is also possible to climb up to the right to a rock ledge via some steps, thereby avoiding the rock step). The gorge walls come closer together again and shortly after two further rock steps have to be overcome. Then the route continues in a leisurely fashion along the bed of the barranco below splendid ivy garlands. After 10 minutes a splendid **rock basin** is reached with numerous cairns. Here the walk ends below a good 10-metre high impassable rock step (waterfall). To the right it is also possible to climb up to the entrance to a gallery.

Canyoning in La Palma: the experience of walking through the Barranco del Agua offers a splendid if short-lived gorge adventure.

13 From Los Tilos to the Mirador de las Barandas and Los Sauces

From the laurel forest to the »banana towns« of the northeast

Los Tilos – Mirador de las Barandas – Los Sauces – Los Tilos

Location: Los Sauces, 266m (bus stop for buses 11 and 12).
Starting point: Los Tilos, 500m. If arriving by bus the walk begins at the turning off to Los Tilos (unofficial bus stop for buses 11 and 12) and ends in Los Sauces.
Walking times: Los Tilos – Mirador de las Barandas ¾ hr (return to Los Tilos from here ½ hr), Mirador de las Barandas – Los Sauces 1¼ hrs, Los Sauces – Los Tilos 1 hr; total time 3 hrs.
Ascent: 600m.
Grade: An easy walk apart from the steep ascent to the Mirador.

Refreshment: Bar-Restaurant in Los Tilos, bars and restaurants in Los Sauces.
Alternative: Descent from Mirador de Llano Clara in the Barranco del Agua: At the Mirador a path forks off to the right along the pipe and drops steeply towards the valley after 30m. At the fork after 5 min, go down left to the canal (5 min). Follow this to the right for a good 5 min and then go through a banana plantation (down to the right to a pylon and then left) to a road in the Barranco del Agua (at Km 1).
Combination possible with Walks 11, 12 and 14.

The attraction of this walk is not only in the splendid views but also in the variety of the landscape, which ranges from laurel forest to banana plantations.

The walk begins directly behind the parking area at the forestry house in **Los Tilos** (sign). First it keeps to the left for a section, and then winds its way steeply up through the laurel forest only interrupted by a few traverses. After nearly three-quarters of an hour – the forest has thinned out a little by now – the path splits. It is still wide enough, and with wooden steps on sections which would otherwise be slippery. Here bear left to the nearby **Mirador de**

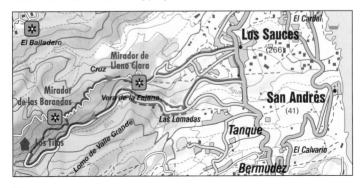

During the descent there are splendid views in the direction of Los Sauces.

las Barandas (shelter, water), which provides a splendid view of the Barranco del Agua, San Andrés and Sauces.

For the walker who does not wish to return to Los Tilos by the same route, the worthwhile descent along the forestry road to Los Sauces is recommended. So go along the track from the viewpoint to the forestry track. This winds gently along the back of the open ground in the direction of Los Sauces and spares the knees. After just under half an hour a paved path goes off to the right from a left-hand bend, thereby cutting off some of the bends and arriving back at the track at the **Mirador de Llano Clara**. From here there is a spectacular view into the Barranco del Agua, down into which a steep sloping path leads (→Alternative). Shortly after a tarmac road is reached which provides a view of the second biggest reservoir basin on the island and leads down to **Los Sauces**, the pretty »banana town« decorated with flowers. In the town stay on the extremely steep road (at a fork bear right) directly to the main square with a church (bars, taxi rank).

Now go right along the main road to the road bridge over the Barranco del Agua (turning to Los Tilos; 20 min). Before the bridge a camino goes off to the right, which stays parallel to the base of the valley and a little above it, and which leads uphill through plantations (stay left at the fork on the way). This ends after a good quarter of an hour in the road to **Los Tilos** next to a bridge. Go along this road for nearly half an hour back to the starting point – a thoroughly charming road walk.

14 From Los Tilos to Barlovento

Varied tranquil high walk in the northeast

Los Tilos (Los Sauces) – Mirador de las Barandas – Galería Meleno – Laguna de Barlovento – Barlovento

Location: Los Sauces, 266m (bus stop for buses 11 and 12).
Starting point: Los Tilos, 500m.
Destination: Barlovento, 548m (bus stop for bus 11).
Walking time: Los Tilos – Mirador de las Barandas ¾ hr, Mirador de las Barandas – Galería Meleno good 1 hr, Galería Meleno – Laguna de Barlovento 1 hr, Laguna de Barlovento – Barlovento good ½ hr; total time 3½ hrs (return walk 3¼ hrs).
Ascent: About 500m of ascent and 450m of descent.

Grade: Strenuous walking (narrow, steep paths; sure-footedness and fitness).
Refreshment: Bar-Restaurant in Los Tilos, bar at the picnic area in Laguna de Barlovento, bars and restaurants in Barlovento.
Alternative: It is also possible to begin the walk in Los Sauces: from the Plaza on the main street go right up the steep road (good 1½ hrs to Mirador de las Barandas; cf also Walk 13).
Combination possible with Walks 12 and 13.

The Parish Church of Los Sauces.

The beautiful, varied connecting path between the towns of Los Sauces and Barlovento is mainly in the shade of the laurel forest, leads past some of the most important water galleries (Galería) and in spring (May, June) has a display of numerous violet flowering Giant Echiums in such quantities and of such beauty as is found nowhere else on La Palma. On the last stage of the walk there is the crater lake of Laguna de Barlovento, a fenced in concrete basin at which a generous-sized picnic area has been built.

Initially the direction of the walk is exactly the same as for Walk 13: the signposted walk begins immediately behind the car park in **Los Tilos** (sign) and leads up steeply through the laurel forest to the **Mirador de las Barandas**, 800m, at which one can take a short

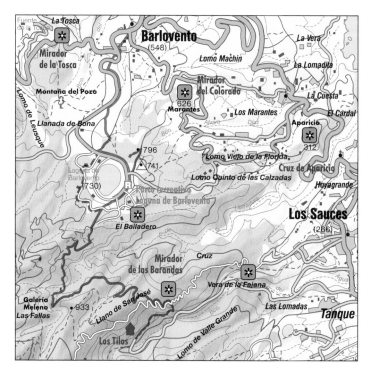

breather. The walk then continues straight on along the forestry track and after 100m turns off left along the wide uphill forestry road, which is left after 10 minutes for a wide foresty track which takes the right-hand fork (straight on). First of all this leads slightly downhill and then more or less contours across the hillside where it is possible to admire whole »forests« of Echiums – the flowering stems of the Giant Echium reach a height of 4 to 5 metres, and it is therefore the largest type of Echium in the Canaries. On the right hand side a beautiful view of Laguna de Barlovento can be enjoyed. After 20 minutes the forestry track goes across a small valley (above numerous Giant Echiums; continue right here along the main track) and leads through a wonderful laurel forest with majestic trees down to the Barranco de la Herradura, one of the most impressive gorges on the island. On past a couple of caves hollowed out of the rock, after half an hour the bottom of the barrranco is reached where the forestry track ends. Shortly after this the

Giant Echium (Pininana).

barranco base is left and one goes up leftwards over a small pile of rubble to a stone house (770m), which is already visible.

To the left of the house the entrance to the **Galería Meleno**, a 4.5km long gallery can be reached via rails. However, go onto the obvious path, which leads rightwards past the house and continues rightwards up through the laurel forest before undulating its way along the hillside. In places it is a bit narrow and steep and slippery if wet, and after a good quarter of an hour it crosses through a side valley with a cataract. Afterwards it goes up steeply for 10 minutes to the mountain ridge above the gorge. Once on top, go straight on up the hill ignoring all of the paths off to the right until after a few minutes the path ends in a forestry track. Go easily downwards along this to the right. After 5 minutes ignore a track which goes off sharply to the right, shortly afterwards taking a second track which also goes off sharply to the right (the straight track goes uphill 50m past the turning off). 5 minutes later a junction is reached where five paths meet together. From here a narrower, defile-like, rather overgrown track goes off left into the scrub. After 5 minutes it ends in a track (walnut tree), which leads up to a plateau. At the next fork (5 min) go right onto the wide track which is abandoned after 50m for a narrow track which leads straight on downwards just before a right-hand bend. A few minutes later this joins a tarmac road at the **Laguna de Barlovento**, 730m.

The crater lake, Laguna de Barlovento, with the summit of the same name in the background.

On the right hand side is the spacious Zona Recreativa Laguna de Barlovento, a well laid out picnic area with barbecue houses, tables and benches, water, football field and campsite – a favourite Palmero destination for excursions. On past the bar it is worth making a detour to a viewpoint with a view of Los Sauces.

Now follow the road in the direction of Barlovento. It leads past the fenced off crater lake and past the foot of a small rise (Laguna de Barlovento, 800m; ascent possible to the right along a track, then sharply left along a path at a high tension mast: 10 min; beautiful view over the artificial lake to the Cumbre). After the slight right-hand bend beyond the lake turn right onto a track, which immediately forks. Keep left and follow the track straight on to the road (10 min) along which the walk continues to the right. Shortly after the hotel La Palma Romántica (nice bar with terrace), there is a short cut on the right via a path (at the fork keep left). A little later the beginning of **Barlovento** is reached. At the Casa Forestal (50m after the left fork on the road which leads to Gallegos) turn right to reach the centre of the town at the main street.

The North

Wild barrancos and an ancient natural landscape

Quiet and cut off, neither playful nor charming is how the harsh north presents itself. It is a landscape filled with mist and light, cut through by wild barrancos and rugged mountain ridges and offering few sites for habitation. There is a shortage of tourist attractions here, the exceptions being a seawater swimming pool (La Fajana near Barlovento) and the picturesquely situated villages of La Tosca, Gallegos and El Tablado which attract the tourists. And on closer acquaintance even the Laguna de Barlovento turns out to be a concrete basin (nowadays, however, filled with water).

One of the best ways of getting to know the north, apart from the well-constructed main road, is the wonderful road from Barlovento to Roque Faro. This gives the wild, deeply forested mountain landscape a free hand. Only rarely are there proper views, but when they occur they are gigantic: the mighty cloud-covered barrancos and the mountain ridges with the bright white houses and the deep-blue ocean in the background. Here nature is reduced to elementals and is completely dominated by the laws of

The Ermita San Antonio del Monte with the Cumbre.

Old mill at Santo Domingo de Garafía.

the wind and weather. This area has to be seen before one realises how endlessly rich it is.

Barlovento, which is well connected to the road network of the island through the main road to Santa Cruz, is a rather sleepy mountain village often shrouded in the trade wind clouds. In the surrounding area there are a number of beautiful walks, some of them waymarked along forestry roads and paths. Further towards the west the sleepy villages of *Gallegos*, *Franceses* and *El Tablado* follow one another, mountain ridge on mountain ridge, only separated from each other by mighty laurel covered barrancos which in places stretch right down almost to the coast. A splendid old royal road connects these villages and Garafía to each other; most impressive is the stretch from the hamlet of La Tosca near Barlovento (wonderful dragon tree grove) to Gallegos and Barranco Fagundo, but the other sections also charm through their wonderful landscape picture. Wonderful walking opportunities are also offered by *Roque Faro*: the small village lies a good 1000m high at the foot of splendid pine forests. The parish of *Santo Domingo de Garafía* is famous for its numerous prehistoric rock carving finds, especially La Zarza and La Zarcita (visitor centre) and for its windmills. The pretty village has a friendly plaza and a romantic port which is reached via a branch road.

15 From Barlovento to Gallegos

Baranco tour through the sleepy north

Mirador La Tosca – La Tosca – La Palmita – Gallegos (– Franceses – El Tablado) and back

Location: Barlovento, 548m (bus stop for bus 11).

Starting point: Mirador La Tosca, 570m (bus stop for bus 11), Look-out platform with palm on the road from Barlovento – Gallegos, parking (just 2km from the church in Barlovento; ½ hr on foot).

Walking time: La Tosca – Gallegos 2½ hrs, return route 2¾ hrs; total time 5¼ hrs.

Ascent: (there and back) good 1000m.

Grade: Generally straightforward but strenuous walking along mainly good tracks – short sections somewhat overgrown. Mainly well marked (white posts, white cross-hairs).

Refreshment: Bar in Gallegos (closed at lunchtime), bars/restaurants in Barlovento.

Alternatives: To somewhat shorten the return route it is possible to ascend to the main road after the Barranco Gallegos (path marked with a white spiral) or after the second large barranco (at transformer tower) and then go back along the road.

Continuation path to Franceses and El Tablado: In Gallegos go down along the village road for ¼ hr until this starts to go upwards towards the left in a bend. Here the paved Camino real to Franceses goes off sharply to the right. After 50m it leads through terraces and then dips back down again. After 10 minutes a very neglected road branches off straight on to Puerto del Gallegos (¼ hr). Go down this to the left. After about ¾ hr the Barranco

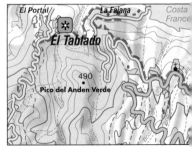

de Franceses is reached, which the path crosses almost at sea level. On the far side it leads up steeply to the road in Franceses. This is followed to the right, whereby in ¼ hr the Plaza in the town district of Los Machines is reached (1¾ hrs from Gallegos; next bus stop for bus 11 on the main road from Barlovento to Roque Faro). 300m later bear right at the crossroads in the direction of La Fajana (sign). The road soon winds down into the Barranco de los Hombres, one of the most impressive gorges on the island (after 25 min a short cut is possible along a camino) and then leads out of the valley to La Fajana. Shortly before the hamlet (1 hr) a track leads off sharply to the left, which goes down into the Barranco de los Hombres. After ¼ hr it becomes a path in the streambed, which after about 50m ascends to the right over a steep mountain ridge to El Tablado (2 hrs from Franceses; bar; no bus connection).

Right near the beginning the path leads through the hamlet of La Tosca.

From **Mirador La Tosca** it is already possible to get an overview of large sections of the walk to Gallegos: directly below lies the dreamy hamlet of La Tosca with its famous dragon tree groves and in the distance it is possible to look over Gallegos towards El Tablado. Do not be deceived by the initial, all too-tame, impression: it is hardly possible from above to see the numerous barrancos which cross this route. A further tip: for anyone who is fit and is not put off by some rather overgrown sections, it is possible to collect further wonderful impressions of the landscape on the continuation path to Franceses and El Tablado – but it is best to organise the return journey before setting out!

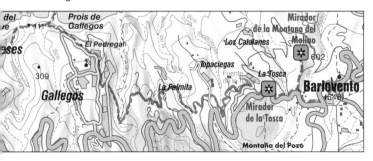

The destination of the walk – the beautifully situated village of Gallegos.

Go along the cemented track, which leads down to the right from the look-out plateau with the palm, and immediately follow the little path that in a few minutes leads directly down to **La Tosca**. It leads to a cemented track: go left onto this. After 5 minutes this in turn ends in a concrete road. Go right along this past a Finca and in the next right-hand bend go straight on along a concrete track, which almost immediately becomes a dirt track, and shortly after becomes a beautiful camino. This leads through the Barranco Topaciegas, which is covered in laurel trees, tree heaths and ferns. Shortly after, the paved path ends in a concrete road, which it leaves again to the right in the next bend. It then descends into the next gorge, the Barranco de la Vica. On climbing back out of the barranco, a rock overhang is passed which serves as a goat shelter. Immediately afterwards, where the path splits, take the left fork straight on. Again the camino ends in a concrete track, which is then followed to the next junction (good 1 hr to this point). Here the camino continues – signs lead through the next mini barranco. On arriving at the other side of the barranco go straight on along the middle track, which leads across the hillside. Rock roses and garden terraces follow, and in a few minutes a clear path leads off left from a right-hand bend. From the next ridge Gallegos can already be seen – so go down into the Barranco de Gallegos. Rock roses are now joined by individual laurel trees, tree heaths and agaves. A gate is passed and then the path finally goes down into the mightiest gorge of the walk. After a further gate the path is in places a bit overgrown (ferns, brambles). Half an hour is needed and then the base of the barranco is reached – it is possible to descend to the sea through the barranco (½ hr, climbing section). In a further quarter of an hour the steep ascent to the first houses of **Gallegos** is over. Here one might not believe one's eyes: another barranco – admittedly a small one – separates one from the actual town. In a good 10 minutes this obstacle is also overcome and one is in the middle of the picturesque, peaceful village (next bus stop for bus 11 on the main road from Barlovento to Roque Faro).

At the entrance to the village of Franceses – in the north of the island goat herds are a frequent sight.

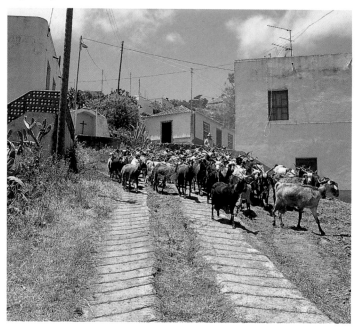

16 From Roque Faro to El Tablado

Strenuous descent on the edge of the Barranco de los Hombres

Roque Faro – El Tablado (– Franceses) and back

Starting point: Bar-restaurant Los Reyes in Roque Faro, 1010m (bus stop for bus 11) on the main road from Santo Domingo de Garafía to Barlovento.
Walking times: Roque Faro – El Tablado 2¼ hrs, El Tablado – Roque Faro 2½ hrs; total time 4¾ hrs.
Ascent: About 700m.
Grade: The walk requires sure-footedness, fitness and a good sense of direction (in places poor, very overgrown paths).
Refreshment: Bar in El Tablado, Bar-restaurants in Roque Faro.
Alternatives: From El Tablado to Franceses (2 hrs): Past the Mirador El Topo is a camino, which splits after 5 min. Here on the right begins the descent into the mighty Barranco de los Hombres. After a good 5 min the beautiful stone-paved royal path leads past a large rock arch, and about 20 min later the base of the gorge is reached (a bit overgrown at the end). Now follow the stream bed to the left for a short section to reach a track, which continues on the right side of the valley in the direction of the sea (after 20m the old Camino real, which is totally overgrown, leads off right to Franceses). After ¼ hr the track ends in a road, which is followed uphill to the right (detour to the left to the nearby beach development La Fajana is possible). After just 10 min an obvious camino marked by white cross-hairs forks off left. It leads up steeply in hairpins and after just ½ hr rejoins the road, which finishes ½ hr later in the village street of Franceses, 460m (telephone to the left after 300m in the square in the Los Machines area of the village; next bus stop for the number 11 bus is on the main road from Barlovento to Roque Faro).

Valley head in the Barranco Carmona.

Descent into the Barranco Carmona / Barranco del Pinalejo (1¼ hrs there and back from the path): The track leads in 25 min to the bottom of the gorge. A path continues up the valley, which after a few minutes ends in a magnificent valley head with a galería and ivy garlands of over 10m in height.
Combination possible with walks 15, 17, 18, 20 and 47.

The old connecting path between Roque Faro and the picturesque village of El Tablado, somewhat neglected in parts, frequently leads through the forest opening up towards the end to give wide views of the north coast. The return path is much easier but not so impressive. Fit walkers can also add on a walk through the impressive Barranco de los Hombres to the neighbouring village of Franceses.

From the Bar-restaurant Los Reyes in **Roque Faro** go down the street to the main road, cross this and go rightwards along the track which leads up onto the mountain ridge (do not branch off downwards to the right). The track passes a threshing area and 100m later a transformer tower. Afterwards it dips down – now partly paved – steeply over the ridge to a cemented track (10 min) which is followed down to the left. Shortly after at the last house it becomes a dirt track, goes for a 100m to the right along the hillside and then leads back down to the left. After 10 min it is necessary to watch out: 15m

past a sharp right-hand bend a track goes off sharply to the left. It leads down through a thickly wooded small valley and after a few minutes goes past a spring. 30m past the spring, the track forks. Bear right to reach a solitary **house** 5 minutes later. Here the track forks again. Go left – to the right of the house – to reach a sharp left-hand bend after about 100m. A narrow forest path (somewhat hidden) goes off sharply to the right from this. It leads slightly downhill across the slope and is in places somewhat overgrown and neglected, but perfectly all right to follow. After a few minutes a path leads off leftwards to the base of the valley: ignore this. Shortly afterwards the track dips down noticeably in zigzags. It soon leads along the top of the mountain ridge from which, however, it soon goes off right to join a track at right angles. Follow this to the left through the small valley, and after a few minutes reach a sharp left-hand bend on the next mountain ridge (the track then leads into the forest reaching the road to El Tablado in a ¼ hr). Here a graded track goes off to the right over the mountain ridge to soon become a steep and very overgrown path. After a short descent on the edge of the scrub it meets up with a camino at right angles, which is followed to the left. The neglected, in parts heavily overgrown path, cuts across the small valley and leads to the other valley side ascending slightly along the slope. After a short descent ignore a path which goes off down to the right. The camino now leads along a wide, heavily overgrown ledge along the precipice above the Barranco de los Hombres and after a few minutes, next to a small well, meets a track on the next mountain ridge. The track is followed to the right, down over the mountain ridge. It is soon cemented and shortly after becomes a fine paved path, which leads past a small stone house after a few minutes. Not long after the house the path leads left towards the barranco. In the bottom of the valley (above a well) it leads for a short distance downhill and then goes left again across the slope. After 10 minutes the track finally ends in the road to El Tablado, which provides the direction for the continuation of the descent.

After 100m at a small stone house, a prominent path crosses the road, (the later return route is left) which is followed down to the right. It soon passes a small reservoir and continues along the edge of the Barranco de los Hombres, whereby it twice skirts the road. At the third bend in the road, continue to walk down along the road into the idyllic village of **El Tablado**, 338m (no bus connection; taxi tel. 922 400103). After about 10 minutes the narrow street forks in the town centre. To the left it is possible to descend to the Barranco Fagundo (→Walk 17). Continue on in the direction of Mirador El Topo, passing the village bar (house no. 59) and shortly after reaching the small look out platform on the roof of the last house, from where there is a magnificent view over the Barranco de los Hombres to the neighbouring village of Franceses.

After a decent rest go back to the small stone house on the road (1.5km from the centre of the village) and walk on uphill along the

The track mainly leads through scrub...

... only at the final ascen doest the view open out to reveal El Tablado and the coast.

beautiful paved track – overgrown in places. In 5 minutes it meets the road again, which is only followed for a few minutes until on the right a cemented track leads off to a cemetery (Cementerio). 30m beyond this the old de-file-like paved path leads off sharply to the left. It meets the road once again after 5 min to abandon it again to the left after 50m before the next right-hand bend. A few minutes later it crosses the road again at a house. At this point the camino becomes a track ending after 20 minutes in a dirt track (possible descent to Barranco Carmona, →Alternative), which leads back up to the road in just 10 minutes (Km 2.3; 868m). Walk on uphill along the little used road. After a quarter of an hour ignore a track which goes off left through a gate. Just 5 minutes later – meanwhile the scrub has been left behind – turn left onto a track. This is somewhat overgrown and leads slightly uphill across the hillside (keep following the main track: go left at the fork after 5 min, immediately after straight on and not right). After a total of 10 min the track joins another track at some large pines. Follow this uphill to the right along the edge of a small valley to meet a track at a house after a few minutes. This is abandoned after 10m for a track which goes off left through the valley. In 5 minutes this leads through wonderful pine forest to cross the main road in **Roque Faro** (school house). After a further 150m the Bar-Restaurant Los Reyes is reached.

17 From El Tablado to Don Pedro

Through perhaps the most beautiful barranco on La Palma

El Tablado – Barranco Fagundo – Don Pedro and back

Starting point: Beginning of El Tablado, 400m (nearest bus stop for bus 11 on the main road from Garafía – Barlovento, from there 6km on good, but steep tarmac roads; in the village there are few places to park so it is best to leave the car at the beginning of the village before the start of the single track concrete road).
Walking time: El Tablado – Barranco Fagundo ¾ hr, Barranco Fagundo – Don Pedro 1½ hrs, return route 2 hrs; total time 4½ hrs.
Ascent: 850m in total.
Grade: Strenuous walking and very sweaty in summer on tracks which are often steep but good. Consider taking swimming costumes for the »beach« at the mouth of the Fagundo (some easy scrambling is however required).

Refreshment: Bar in El Tablado.
Alternative: Continuation of the walk to Santo Domingo de Garafía (bus stop for buses 5 and 11, →Walk 20).
Combination possible with Walks 16 and 18.

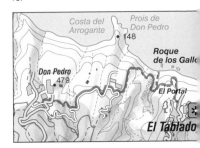

El Tablado, picturesquely situated on a broad ridge of land between the deep gorges of the Barranco Fagundo and the Barranco de los Hombres is one of the most beautiful and typical villages on La Palma. Here begins one of the most impressive walks on the island: through the Barranco Fagundo.
Walk down along the concrete road surface between the gardens and houses, passing a washing place and go straight on until a signposted paved way goes off to the left. It leads at first down the ridge of land and then goes left towards the **Barranco Fagundo**. The steeper sections of the royal way are here and there a bit unpleasant to walk. After three quarters of an hour the

The camino through the Barranco Fagundo spoils the walker with its lush xerophytic vegetation and magnificent view of the sea.

bottom of the Barranco is reached, only 5 metres above sea level. To reach where the gorge joins the sea is only 5 minutes from here (an adventurous excursion: the last rock steps to the narrow strip of sand are overcome with the help of a primitive wooden ladder).

On the other side it goes up steeply towards the top. The path curves into a side valley with an indescribable variety of xerophytic plants and then takes a wide bend to climb the mountain shoulder with fantastic deep views of the coastal cliffs. As soon as the edge of the Barranco is reached, this is followed to the top, until finally after an hour (from the bottom of the Barranco) a man-sized stone pillar with engravings fixed in the stone is reached – a splendid look out point! – followed by a solitary farmhouse 50m further on. From here a concrete road leads on upwards in the direction of La Zarza. However follow the track which goes off to the right, and leads in 25 minutes (after a ¼ hr, at the latest before the hairpin bend, continue rightwards on the clear, sometimes overgrown camino) to the Plaza of **Don Pedro**, 470m, with the school house which can be seen from a long way off.

18 From La Zarza to Don Pedro

Magnificent, adventurous descent through rain-forest barrancos

Parque Cultural La Zarza – Barranco de La Zarza – Barranco Magdalena – Don Pedro (– El Tablado)

Starting point: Parque Cultural La Zarza, 1000m (bus stop for bus 11), on the main road from Santo Domingo de Garafía to Roque Faro, at the hamlet of San Antonio del Monte.

Walking time: Parque Cultural La Zarza – Suspension bridge 1 hr, Suspension bridge – Don Pedro (Plaza) 2 hrs, return route 3¾ hrs; total time 6¾ hrs.

Ascent: About 600m.

Grade: Generally good, not difficult walking apart from a climbing section in the Barranco Magdalena. As it partly goes along a streambed it is best avoided after rain (water in the stream now and then).

Combination possible with Walks 17 and 20.

Advice: The Parque Cultural La Zarza is

Start of the rain forest adventure.

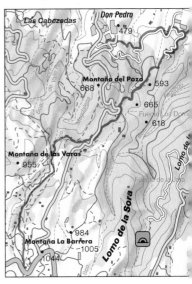

open on Tues–Sat 11–17.00 and Sun 12–18.00. Don Pedro does not have a bus connection; it is also possible to walk back along the little-used road to La Zarza (5km).

This walk through the still almost untouched laurel forest of the Barranco La Zarza and the Barranco Magdalena is a secret tip for nature lovers with a sense of adventure. It promises a rainforest experience of the highest order and is one of the most beautiful and impressive walks on the island.

In the impressive Barranco de la Zarza.

From the building of the **Parque Cultural La Zarza** go along the vehicle track, which goes under the main road via a tunnel. Shortly after the tunnel there is a left-hand bend in the track (small rock wall with caves) from which a narrow walking track leads off to the left and which leads along the bed of the Barranco de la Zarza. 5 minutes later the path, which is marked with red dots, meets a track. Follow this to the right and then leave it immediately in the following right hand bend to go along the stepped path to the left. This leads down into a fantastic basin, which nature could not have more beautifully modelled: pure rainforest, with ivy, which twines down from the dense leaf canopy to the base of the barranco. At the head of the valley after rainfall there is a small waterfall. The small valley now provides the continuation of the walk. After a few minutes the path joins up again with a track along which are apple tree espalier. The track ends, however, a few minutes later: continue here along the forest path. Shortly afterwards this switches over to the other side of the valley (bridge), climbs upwards for a short distance and then afterwards dips down into a broader even more impressive valley basin. Before the path completely descends into the barranco bottom it leads in a semi-circle through the crag on the rear side of the basin. After, it crosses over the streambed (bridge) to lead on down along the right-hand side of the valley above the deeply incut barranco. After a short section up and down (do not go off to the right) the track dips down into a third, no less beautiful basin and switches over to the left side of the valley (bridge, waterfall and gallery at the valley head). 20m after the bridge, the track forks, (the main track straight on leads to San Antonio del Monte, →Walk 19). Stay to the right in the streambed and immediately afterwards pass an enclosed spring. A good 5 minutes later a small rock step is reached, which is avoided by a path on the right-hand side of the valley (15m back). 50 metres later the bed of the stream, which sometimes has some water, is regained. Without any real obstacle it is possible to continue walking along/next to the streambed of the Barranco Magdelena, until after 10 minutes the track forks. Whoever wants a test of courage can go straight on for 25m and cross the gorge via a **suspension bridge**. You can however dispense with this dubious pleasure and cross to the path on the right side of the streambed. Shortly after, the route returns to the streambed. After 10 minutes the wood suddenly thins out for a few metres. The path now dips down over a rock step (easy scrambling) to the streambed in order to carry on again on the

Scrambling section in the Barranco Magdalena.

right side of the valley. A few minutes later the stretch through the gorge comes to an end: a path goes off to the left but stay on the straight path, which leads up steeply on the right-hand side of the valley. After about 10 minutes a charca (cave with a spring) is passed on the right of the track, which now noticeably flattens and undulates across the slope. Shortly after, a water trough with a tap is passed. 2 minutes later the path splits – go straight on (right) along the main track, which shortly after ends in the road to Don Pedro (2.5km from La Zarza) immediately next to a plaza with an oratorium of San Miguel.

Follow the road down to the left and in the following bend next to the irrigation ditch go straight on (right) along the track (Camino Cambao)

View from the descent path towards Juan Adalid and its wind turbines.

which goes downwards parallel to the road. It soon becomes a wide paved road and ends after 10 minutes in a track, which leads to the left to the road. In the bend in the road a clear path forks off, which after a short steep descent becomes a beautiful camino. After just 10 minutes a water trough is passed (5m right of the path). At this point the path is a bit overgrown. Gradually this becomes a track, which is left again just 10 minutes after the trough in a sharp left-hand bend along a continuation path which goes straight on (along water pipes). At the fork after 10m keep straight on. It leads easily across the slope on the left side of the crest and forks again 5 minutes later (to the left after 50m a small rise with a water reservoir is reached from which there is a splendid view of Don Pedro and towards the wind generators of Juan Adalid, with the Cumbre and its observatory behind one). At this fork stay to the right on the main path, thereby reaching the mountain ridge after a few minutes at the foot of which is the Barranco Fagundo. Now it is not far down to the first houses of the eastern part of Don Pedro. Shortly after the first house a track is reached, which (soon cemented) leads to a farmhouse. Here go left to the track (straight on it is possible to descend to Barranco Fagundo and onwards to El Tablado, →Walk 20). It leads in 25 minutes to the Plaza of **Don Pedro**, 470m, with the white schoolhouse visible from a long way off, above it (after ¼ hr, and in any case before the hairpin bend, go right along the obvious if partly overgrown camino).

19 From La Zarza to the Ermita San Antonio

Short, easy circuit through the splendid Barranco de La Zarza

Parque Cultural La Zarza – Barranco de La Zarza – Ermita San Antonio del Monte – Parque Cultural La Zarza

Starting point: Parque Cultural La Zarza, 1000m (bus stop for bus 11) on the main road from Santo Domingo de Garafía – Roque Faro, at the hamlet of San Antonio del Monte.
Walking time: Parque Cultural La Zarza – Ermita San Antonio 1¼ hrs, return route 40 min; total time 2 hrs.
Ascent: About 200m.
Grade: Easy walking which requires some surefootedness – watch out carefully for turnings off.
Alternative: From the Ermita San Antonio to Garafía or to Llano Negro: 50m opposite the entrance to the chapel a track leads off in a westerly direction from the approach road. It leads along under the transmitting station summit of San Antonio up to a rise (5 min; straight on at the junction) and down on the other side. After a total of 15 min in a sharp left-hand bend a somewhat neglected camino, which is accompanied by a water pipe, leads off to the right. It goes downhill between pines and soon crosses the track. A little later at a couple of houses it meets the track again, which is followed to the left through the Barranco de la Luz (left Fuente de la Hiedra). At the next mountain ridge (40 min from Ermita) a forestry track joins

it from the left, which leads directly up to Llano Negro (good ½ hr, camino in parts; bus stop for buses 5 and 11). To go on to Garafía turn right at this point onto the somewhat overgrown path. It soon turns out to be a beautiful old paved way and after 20 min becomes a cemented track at the first houses. Some minutes later at a washing place it joins a paved road, which leads down to the Plaza de Santa Domingo de Garafía (1½ hrs from Ermita; bus stop for buses 5 and 11).
Combination possible with walk 18.
Tip: Before or after the walk one should not miss out on visiting the Parque Cultural La Zarza (open Tue–Sat 11–17.00 and Sun 12–18.00): A fine walk through the archaeological park leads to the prehistoric rock etchings of La Zarza (above Fuente de la Zarza) and La Zarcita (in a side valley to the right of the spring).

This beautiful leisurely walk offers itself for those who do not want to take on the long strenuous descent to Don Pedro, but nevertheless, would like to get to know the charming Barranco de La Zarza.
Initially the walk from **Parque Cultural La Zarza** through the Barranco de La Zarza is identical with →Walk 18 (see there). At the fork in the path in the third valley basin stay on the main path straight on, which now leads to the left side of the valley. 20 minutes later the camino splits again – here keep right. The path goes up along the slope and meets a track on a rise after 10 minutes. Follow this to the left, keep right at the fork after 100m and at the next fork after a further 100m go left. 30m later there is a crossing of paths.

Go straight on here and bear left after 10m along the beautiful camino. After a good 5 minutes this meets up with the road to Juan Adalid. On the other side is an unsurfaced road, which – always straight on – ends after a good 5 minutes in the approach road to the Ermita San Antonio del Monte (15m before the road, the continuation path for the later part of the walk goes off to the left). Go right through the wide gap in the wall to reach a huge open area on which a leisure park with barbecue huts has been set up (Parque de Ocio y Natureleza de San Antonio del Monte). At the end of the area is the **Ermita San Antonio del Monte**, 910m.

After a visit to the chapel go over the long leisure park back to the gap in the wall (5 min), cross the unsurfaced road and follow the track which leads up parallel to the road into a small valley. After a few minutes the track forks – go straight on here. 2 minutes later a camino bears off to the left, which in 5 minutes leads over to the road to Juan Adalid. Opposite, a track leads off to the right past a couple of houses. It crosses through a small valley and forks on the next mountain ridge. On this and the next fork after another 100m go straight on. The track now dips down into the Barranco de La Zarza. After 5 minutes a sharp left-hand bend in the bottom of the barranco is reached. Here the camino, which is familiar from the approach walk, branches off sharply to the right, leading back through the valley and the tunnel to the **Parque Cultural La Zarza** (10 min).

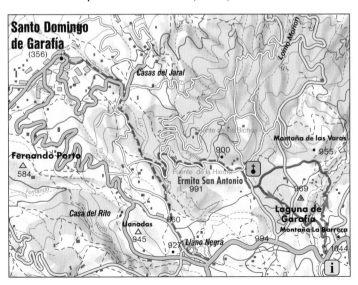

Immediately after the last houses the Camino real leads down into the bottom of the Barranco El Palmar. Watch out for the waymarks (white cross-hairs) and cairns on the climb back out through the steep, rocky terrain with cacti, otherwise going wrong is a certainty. On arriving at the top a white house is passed and a track is crossed. The camino is obvious once again – it leads to the right of a farmhouse with palm trees and shortly after joins a track, which is abandoned in the following right-hand bend along the path forking off to the left. Shortly after it meets a track again, along which the next barranco is crossed. Above the hamlet of **El Mudo** the track splits. Keep to the right here and go onto the paved path, which goes off to the left in the next right-hand bend. After a few minutes it leads past an enclosed spring with a water collection basin. Shortly afterwards, the Barranco de Domingo Díaz, the most impressive barranco of the walk so far, appears. Beyond this on the next large ridge the wind turbines of Juan Adalid, on the next stage of the walk, can already be seen. After a short 10 minute traverse of the hillside the base of the gorge is reached (gate). Afterwards the camino ascends in zigzags to the next plateau (¼ hr). On arriving at the top go through the gate and follow the path, which is bordered by tree heaths. Straight away it crosses a track and leads over to the ridge of land of **Juan Adelid**, 500m. Go to the right past the first house and cross the road which leads to San Antonio del Monte and go straight on along the track which leads between the wind turbines. Immediately after the next right-hand bend a camino, which leads off left by a power mast, is ignored. A few minutes later the track leads past a house standing on its own. Directly above the house on a rise the waymarked Camino real forks off right. It leads between tree heath bushes across the hillside and forks after 5 minutes. Go right here along the main path. Now a first, indistinct barranco is crossed which can be rather overgrown in parts. After crossing the barranco the path splits just before a pylon. Stay, however, on the straight level path to reach a ridge (gate, cross), to which a path descending from San Antonio del Monte leads. Now Don Pedro can be seen ahead and the view upwards reaches as far as the Roque de los Muchachos. Continue straight on along the camino, which now leads into the Barranco de Valle Rey. After a good 5 minutes a couple of small houses are passed. Leave these behind to the left and finally descend completely down into the base of the gorge (¼ hr). There are a few laurel trees here, and brambles twine down from the trees and the rock walls. The path here can be very overgrown in places and is steep in parts. It now goes up steeply for a short distance on the other side and then leads left along a ledge through the cliffs to the first houses of **Don Pedro**, 470m (20 min). Here a cemented track is crossed and the track which leads across the slope is followed. This leads in 5 minutes to the road with the Plaza and the schoolhouse. 25m before the schoolhouse the camino real goes off to the right from the Plaza towards El Tablado. It goes

El Tablado, the destination of the walk.

down a short section with steps and then goes easily across the hillside, forking after a good 5 minutes. Stay on the path, which goes straight on and joins a track a few minutes later. This leads in 10 minutes over to the next large ridge, where it goes to the right past a farmhouse with dragon trees. 5 minutes later the track ends at a last farmhouse just before the Barranco Fagundo. Here a wide path continues over the ridge, after 50m passing a stone pillar as high as a person with a rock engraving set in the stone – a splendid look out point with a fine view of El Tablado and of the continuation of the route. About 10 minutes later the path arrives at a point directly above the cliffs, which drop away vertically. The camino now turns to the right towards the Barranco Fagundo and descends into the mighty gorge in numerous zigzags. After about 20 minutes a large dark-coloured overhang with numerous caves is passed. A few minutes later the base of the barranco is reached. Here a short exciting detour to the Playa is worthwhile (¼ hr there and back): the path leads directly along the bed of the barranco hemmed in on both sides by rock walls; the final rock step to the narrow strip of sand is overcome with the help of a primitive wooden ladder. Afterwards climb up the camino real to **El Tablado**. Keep following the main path to reach the village road, which forks 5 minutes later. Here take the road to the left in the direction of the Mirador El Topo (sign) which leads to the village bar (house number 59) from where one can call a taxi (Tel 922 40 01 03).

The West

Idyllic beaches, plantations and impressive lava landscapes

Puerto Naos is the tourist centre of the west coast.

»La Palma's sunnyside« is the advertising slogan used for the west of the island, and indeed the region between Puerto de Tazacorte and Puerto Naos has the most hours of sunshine on the island, and, what the holidaymakers probably like the most: the nicest beaches. The reliable climate with little rain in the lee of the Cumbres does, however, have its down side: the vegetation is not so lush as on the east coast and the coastal region is dominated by an incomparable monoculture, with banana plantations as far as the eye can see.

The fertile and heavily populated Valle de Aridane with the towns of *Los Llanos de Aridane* and *El Paso* form the economic backbone of the island. Not without reason Los Llanos is frequently called the »secret capital« of La Palma. Less so on account of the sight seeing attractions, for apart from the invitingly pretty Plaza España, it does not have much to offer, but more because the most productive plantations are in this area, and the tourist perspective is right. In particular this is the case with *Puerto Naos*, which apart from Los Cancajos, is the most significant and indeed most attractive bathing resort of the island, if one ignores the indiscriminately high apartment block complexes behind the beach promenade. Immediately to the south of the town two of the finest sandy bays of La Palma are found: Playa de las Monjas (only nude beach on the island) and Charco Verde. These are almost as good as the Playa Nueva to the north of Puerto Naos. A further highlight of the area is the charming little town of Tazacorte with its cosy plaza. This also applies to *Puerto de Tazacorte* – although not unqualified, as neither the stony beach nor the frightful concrete buildings fit its unique position at the mouth of the mightiest gorge of the island: the Barranco de las Angustias which leads down from the Caldera de Taburiente.

Almost 600m higher up, right on the top of a cliff, the Mirador El Time has the complete Aridane Valley and the west coast at its feet. The view along the Barranco de las Angustias into the Caldera de Taburiente is alone worth stopping off for at this look out point. Now the landscape changes – numerous barrancos cut through the slopes of the Caldera, the coast becomes more rugged and inaccessible. Even the plantations become less frequent and are replaced with terraces with almond trees (mainly neglected) and the ever-lower spreading pine forests which cover the otherwise mainly barren landscape. On past *Tijarafe*, which with its rocky bay of Porís de Candelaria, possesses the most spectacular natural port of the island, *Puntagorda* is reached. Just before the beginning of the town it is worth visiting the twin dragon trees. Apart from this the town, which is rather spread out, is renowned for its almond blossom festival, which usually takes place at the beginning of February. In the Puerto a small beach with a natural swimming pool awaits the visitor. On the other side of the Barranco de Izcague with its tranquil dragon tree grove village of *Las Tricias* it leads on past the rich green meadow slopes to the Hoya Grande and thereby to the northern part of the island.

The Playa de la Veta on the spectacular precipitous northwest coast.

21 From Las Tricias to the Buracas Caves

Easy circuit through dragon tree groves and flowering gardens

Las Tricias – Buracas and back

Starting point: Church at the beginning of Las Tricias, 700m (bus stop for bus 5), 1km from the main road Punta Gorda – Hoya Grande on the side road to Santa Domingo de Garafía.

Walking time: Descent to the Buracas Caves good ¾ hr, return route nearly 1 hr; total time 1¾ hrs.

Ascent: About 250m.

Grade: Easy village paths.

Refreshment: Bar opposite the church.

Alternatives: Through the Barranco de Izcague (40 min): 10 minutes below the church, right next to the turning off into the first street, a camino goes off left. Follow this between two houses (archaeological collection on right) and straight on along the unsurfaced road. A water tank is reached after 15 minutes, past which a camino leads down into the Barranco de Izcague (splendid vegetation; ¼ hr) and up the other side to the main road to Puntagorda (10 min).

From Buracas to Punta de Hiscaguán (¾ hr): Past the caves and prehistoric rock etchings a narrow, steep camino leads up. It passes a cave house (left here at the fork) and ends after 10 minutes in an unsurfaced road. Along this to the left in a wide right-hand bend down to a solitary farm (20 min; shortcut possible along a

path). A path goes left along the edge of the drop to the Barranco de Izcague (take care!). It immediately goes through a gate and leads through a very romantic area with giant fig cactus trees, at least 3m high. After a good ¼ hr, bear leftwards to a weakly defined rock spur, from which a splendid view of the rocky coast can be had.

Combination possible with Walk 22.

In the area of **Las Tricias** one can experience the perfect La Palma. Lush gardens, delightful dragon tree groves and the ever-present view of the wide ocean characterise this landscape blessed by nature, and this walk goes throught the middle of this paradise.

First of all go down along the road for about 15 min (do not take the

Pleasant walk between dragon trees and the deep-blue ocean – Las Tricias.

road off to the left after 10 min) until a track bears off left from a right-hand bend after the point where the road narrows to a single track. Here the partly paved track leads over the ridge, soon becoming a tarmac road, and after 5 minutes it leads past the Casa Blanca. Shortly after, the road swings to the right away from the ridge. Fork left here (straight on) along a wide path. It passes a round threshing place and leads with a view of the Barranco de Izcague further on down the ridge to a track, which goes left immediately past an old gofio (roasted maize meal) mill on a knoll (½ hr). Stay on the track which now curves over to a small barranco. After just 15 minutes it splits 10m before a water reservoir. Here bear right to the dragon trees in the bottom of the valley, through which a fine path continues. At the next branch in the path, keep to the left downhill and then immediately on the path to the right. This leads in a few minutes to the **Cuevas de Buracas**, 400m. The caves themselves are not very spectacular, but the drawings on the rocks are interesting. Follow the path past the caves for about 30m, until on the right a path goes off over some blocks to the upper caves. Here there are engravings on some of the rocks.

From the caves go back along the path onto the ridge and follow the fine path up to the left (at a fork continue sharply left along the paved path) with a view of the barranco and the caves. Soon a grove of dragon trees is passed. Keep straight on along the uphill paved path, which soon becomes an un-surfaced road and shortly afterwards crosses another unsurfaced road. Finally it becomes a path again, ending at the threshing place in the path used on the descent. Go back along this to the church.

In rough seas the water boils and foams everywhere on the Lomada Grande point.

further on a path with blue waymarks, which is at first somewhat unclear, goes off to the right between rows of stones towards Lomada Grande. The old camino, paved in parts, leads down between rock roses and pines and after a few minutes crosses the right side of the small valley. Afterwards the path leads for a short while on the following ridge to then lead to the right towards the next valley characterised by its gardens. Here the camino only goes down for a few minutes before it splits. At this point do not go left, but continue straight on over to the next ridge, which is descended keeping slightly to the right. Keep following the blue line markings, crossing a track after 5 minutes and a small valley to the right. Shortly after on the next ridge go through a meadow gate and then keep going down to the right of the three pines towards a large eucalyptus tree in the right section of the small valley and a pretty estate. Just before the eucalyptus tree the camino goes across the small valley to join a track on the next ridge next to the estate. From the house a track leads on down. After about 100m (above pines) this is abandoned for a path which leads down into the bottom of the valley. On the next ridge next to a large **estate** a track is joined again which is followed downwards. It soon ends to the left on a platform – straight on an old camino continues, in places overgrown/derelict. It continues on down over the ridge, so there are no navigational problems. Shortly after the end of the track, go through a field gate, from which there is a splendid view of the

rocky coast and the Lomada Grande point. 10 minutes later the camino leads to the right along a fence. Below this is now an unsurfaced road from which a path also leads down to Lomada Grande. The continuation is now first on the ridge and only near the drop to the Lomada Grande does it turn right towards the hillside (do not go too near to the edge as the wall is overhanging in places and prone to landslips!) Shortly after, next to a well, it joins the path coming down from the unsurfaced road. The camino now descends in wide hairpins, sometimes protected by rails, down through the precipice to **Lomada Grande**. It passes a number of houses built into the rock face and finally ends in a spacious cave in which boats are kept. When the sea is rough this offers a magnificent natural spectacle, especially in the rock holes on the flat lava promontory in which the water foams up and down. When the sea is calm it is possible to take a refreshing swim in one of the natural swimming pools or in the sheltered bay in front of the cave.

After the walk an excursion to the beaches to the north of Lomada Grande is an attractive proposition.

23 Playa de Garome

Short, easy descent to the beach colony of Tinizara

Tinizara – Playa de Garome and back

Location: Tinizara, 890m (bus stop for bus 5), in the parish of Tijarafe on the road to Puntagorda.
Starting point: From the main road in Tinizara next to the supermarket Celia, about 100m to the north of the bar-restaurant Tinizara, a narrow road goes off (it leads past the church after 50m). After 7km, at a height of about 300m the road becomes a track at a point between banana plantations where the car can be parked.
Walking time: End of the tarmac – Playa de Garome ¾ hr, return route nearly 1 hr; total time 1¾ hrs (from Tinizara an extra 3½ hrs there and back).
Ascent: 300m.
Grade: Short, easy walk along paths which in places are rather narrow and steep, thus requiring sure-footedness.
Refreshment: None en route. Bar-restaurant in Tinizara.
Alternative: From the Playa de Garome to Playa Camariño (and to Puntagorda): From the beach a narrow and at first somewhat neglected cliff path leads off in a northerly direction. It leads right along the foot of the cliff and should

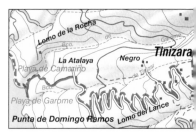

only be undertaken by fit mountain walkers with a head for heights and when the weather is settled (stonefall danger!). After a good 10 minutes of laborious up and down, including easy scrambling the stony beach of Playa Camariño below an overhanging cliff is reached. After this the path climbs a bit again and splits a few minutes later. To the left a path leads down to a bay with underground springs at the mouth of the Barranco de Roque. The right-hand path goes through a short tunnel after 50m and at a plantation joins a minor road, along which one can go on up to Puntagorda (2–3 hrs).

Every place on the northwest coast has its »puertito« and beach – each one more beautiful than its neighbour and each incredibly romantic in its own distinct way. Tinizara's beach is at the mouth of the Barrranco de Garome, which runs down to the sea immediately to the north of the small town. It even has a small strip of sand, which is highly suitable for bathing when the sea is calm. In the vertical cliffs on either side of the barranco mouth a number of simple weekend houses have been built, some of which have pretty front gardens.

About 10 minutes from the end of the tarmac, the steep track, cemented in places, ends at a small **turning point** in front of a banana plantation (about 200m high). Here a path protected by a railing begins on the right and leads down into the Baranco de Garome. Soon the first views down to the cliffs

Descent into the extremely romantic Barranco de Garome.

can be gained; then, the camino, which in places is extremely steep, leads rightwards towards the hillside. After about 20 minutes comes the most beautiful section: go through a rock arch and past an overhanging cliff. The bright coloured layers in the heavily undercut cliffs of the gorge are particularly interesting, and these can be carefully studied during the course of the descent. A little above the beach the path crosses the base of the barranco to finally lead down to the **Playa de Garome** at the other side of the valley. Before the stony beach the path splits. To the right, on past the cave dwellings, it is possible to make an excursion to Playa Camariño (→Alternative). To the left, right next to the beach, a cemented path leads over to an underground spring (Pozo de Garome) and to further weekend bungalows. Beyond is the narrow sandy beach, which according to the time of year only comes into the sun at midday or in the afternoon, and is, moreover, very prone to stonefall.

24 Playa de la Veta

Short descent to one of La Palma's most beautiful beaches

Tijarafe – Playa de la Veta and back

Location: Tijarafe, 663m (bus stop for bus 5).

Starting point: Parking area, 150m, above Playa de la Veta.

Approach drive:
a) From the middle of Tijarafe follow the main road to Puntagorda for 300m until on the left the Calle Accesso al Colegio branches off. Follow this straight on downwards, crossing another road. After 1.6km the road forks at an irrigation canal – go right here along the canal (the road which goes straight on leads down in the direction of Playa de las Vinagreras). After a further 1.6km the extremely narrow and steep road to Playa de la Veta goes off left ending at a small car park after 2.7km.

b) Opposite the Bar La Guaga, 830m on the main road from Tijarafe – Puntagorda (2.5km from Tijarafe; bus stop for bus 5) a

road leads off towards the sea which is followed straight on. After 2.8km it leads to the left at a canal and 250m further on the road to the car park goes off to the right (2.7km).

Walking time: Car park – Playa la Veta ½ hr, return route 40 min; total time just 1¼ hrs (from Tijarafe or Bar La Guaga an extra 3 hrs there and back).

Ascent: 160m.

Grade: Short, easy walk along a well-constructed path which however does require sure-footedness in parts (torch for the tunnel may be useful).

Refreshment: Bar-restaurants in Tijarafe and Bar La Guaga.

Advice: Playa de la Veta can also be reached by boat: these start from Puerto de Tazacorte.

In the past Playa de la Veta could only be approached – other than from the sea – via an extremely exposed path through cliffs. Since the building of a pedestrian tunnel, however, this hidden dream beach has also become accessible to the »normal« walker, and without the need for excessive exertion. So the once secret tip will no doubt have a similar future to the neighbouring »pirate bay«, which is also published for the first time in this walking guide.

A perfect paradise – Playa de la Veta.

From the **car park** at the end of the approach road a wide somewhat rocky path starts, which soon provides a good view of the rugged coast. After 5 minutes the camino leads through a tunnel of about 30m in length, which can be negotiated without a torch provided there is sufficient daylight (watch out for projections on the roof at head height!). After, the camino (at this point protected by a railing) goes for a short section through the cliff and down steps, steep and between cliffs in places, to the **Playa de la Veta**. All around this splendid bathing bay, which is about 100m long and enclosed by giant boulders and scree at both ends and a cliff behind, there are numerous bungalows with brightly coloured gardens. This idyllic weekend colony even has a Plaza shaded by large rubber trees on which boats are laid up in winter.

Those who wish to explore can go off and get to know the coast at the foot of the mighty cliffs, which are up to 400m in height. Particularly worthwhile is an excursion to the north to the mooring place for the boats and onwards to a second, somewhat smaller sandy beach.

25 From Tijarafe to the »Pirate Bay«

Unique: the massive rock overhang with the weekend bungalows

Tijarafe – Barranco del Jurado – Playa del Jurado – Porís de Candelaria – Tijarafe

Starting point: Centre of Tijarafe, 663m, (bus stop for number 5 bus), or 600m along the route (see below).

Walking time: Tijarafe – Road of El Jesús ¾ hr, Road of El Jesús – Playa del Jurado 1 hr, Playa del Jurado – Porís de Candelaria ¾ hr, Porís de Candelaria – Tijarafe 1¾ hrs; total time 4¼ hrs.

Ascent: 850m.

Grade: Long, strenuous walk on paths which are sometimes narrow, steep and rocky, thus requiring absolute sure-footedness. For the tunnel a torch is required. Very hard work if hot!

Refreshment: Bars and restaurants in Tijarafe.

Alternative: Direct descent to the Pirate bay (1½ hrs): At the junction after 10 min keep following the steeply descending road (20 min after the banana plantation, keep right at the fork and follow a paved way for 10 min where the road ends); it is also possible to follow the road rightwards to the next ridge (nearly 5 min) and walk down the ridge (direction unclear in places, watch out for cairns; see return route).

Advice: It is best to visit the »pirate bay« from midday onwards once the sun has made its way into this over-dimensional hiding place, and do not forget swimming costumes.

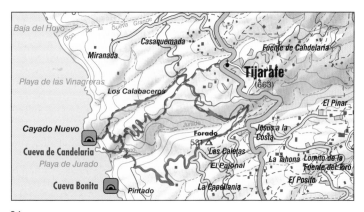

The Playa del Jurado: the Cueva Bonito is right next to this.

There is hardly any other mightier and more impressive place on the coast of the »Isla Bonita« than this unique rocky bay: a fantastic, natural concert hall with a long rock colossus in the middle. In the giant, nearly 50-metre high rock overhang are built nearly two-dozen rock houses, almost a small village – purely functional houses for fishermen and weekends. Nevertheless nothing is missing: light bulbs hang from the electric cables in the gloomy cave, a sink, toilets, their own mooring place in the furthest corner, everything is there which belongs to a Puerto in La Palma.

Immediately to the north of the centre of **Tijarafe** a steep concrete road goes off next to the Spar shop (Sign: »Guardia Civil«) and leads down the mountain ridge. After 600m (10 min) it becomes a tarmac road and cuts across a track at this point (20m afterwards on the right of the road there is a small white tower with good parking spots).

From here it is possible to descend directly to the pirate bay (→Alternative). However, to follow the main walk, go left at the junction along the track. In a good 5 minutes this leads to a tunnel (paled gate, pipe) where the torch is required for the first time. After about 5 minutes the tunnel ends in the cliff of the mighty **Barranco del Jurado**. Follow the path which more or less con-

tours along next to the pipe, crossing the base of the barranco to the other side of the valley where it goes through four more tunnels in quick succession. For the last of these tunnels the torch is needed again – it takes about 5 minutes to go through it (after a few minutes there is a window in the tunnel which allows a view of the cemetery of Tijarafe). 25 metres after the tunnel turn sharply to the left along a track, which immediately joins one of the roads coming down from El Jesús. Go down to the left along this. After about 7 minutes a first sharp left-hand bend is reached; a few minutes later there is a further left-hand bend in which a pista – first cemented then with a tarmac surface – goes off to the right (Pista del Jurado). This leads in a few minutes past a paradise-like garden, which belongs to the estate of the famous composer Frank Duval. After a total of a good 20 minutes a large round reservoir is reached in a sharp left-hand bend (splendid view of the rugged coast with Playa del Jurado). About 40m before this, next to a small well, a track goes off right, which leads down parallel to the marked out route of a rusty material cable car into the Barranco del Jurado. After a good 5 minutes an oratorium is passed and a good 5 minutes later it passes a cable car support. Here the unpleasant steep scree path goes off left from the cable car route and dips down completely to the base of the gorge where a couple of weekend houses have been built in the cliffs. Before continuing the ascent on the other side of the valley go to the stony **Playa del Jurado** – somewhat to the south and not visible from here is the most famous sea grotto of the island, the Cueva Bonita, which can be reached by swimmers with good stamina when the sea is absolutely calm.

Then go along the base of the barranco up to the last buildings, where an underground spring is found (Pozo Jurado: in the past the water was transported up to the plantations using the cable car). In front of the buildings a staircase leads up to the last little house, past which a scree path continues. It winds its way up steeply and after nearly half an hour it ends on a ridge in a cemented track, which is followed downwards to the left. After a good 5 minutes the minor road ends and a paved path continues. It crosses over the

Even in the afternoon the huts in the bay are still in the shadow of the overhang.

Barranco del Pueblo (after a few minutes the later return path bears off to the right) and leads in 10 minutes to the mighty rocky bay of **Porís de Candelaria**, whose turquoise-coloured pool invites one to a swim when the sea is calm.

Enjoy the unique atmosphere and wait on sunny days before returning until the heat of the day has passed. Initially follow the approach route and after a good 5 minutes at the end of the cliff to the left of the path, go off sharply left along the camino mentioned above. This passes a couple of cave dwellings and goes up steeply on the left side of the valley of the Barranco del Pueblo near the back of the ridge. After about 40 minutes one is at the level of the first overgrown terraced fields. Now the path becomes unclear – so watch out carefully for cairns which indicate the best line of ascent. The path runs first of all to the right of the valley base along the edge of the terrace walls and gradually makes its way rightwards towards the ridge, which is ascended in a direct line. After nearly half an hour Tijarafe appears, and the small white tower from the approach walk can also be seen. Another good 5 minutes on the edge of the narrow, rocky ridge, then a diagonal track is met. In 5 minutes this goes to the right over to the road by the white tower. This leads back to the left to **Tijarafe**.

26 Hoya Grande and Torre del Time, 1160m

Spectacular look out tower on the edge of the drop to the Angustias Gorge

El Jesús – El Pinar – Hoya Grande – Torre del Time – El Pinar – El Jesús

Starting point: El Jesús, 610m (bus stop for bus 5), bus stop at Km 67.5 on the main road from Mirador El Time – Tijarafe (opposite a paved square on the seaward side; about 250m before this a picnic area with parking).

Walking time: El Jesús – El Pinar ¾ hr, El Pinar – Torre del Time 1¾ hrs, Torre del Time – El Pinar 1¼ hrs, El Pinar – El Jesús ¾ hr; total time 4½ hrs.

Ascent: Altogether about 1000m.

Grade: Strenuous mountain walking, possible navigation problems.

Alternative: Descent from Torre del Time to Mirador El Time or to La Punta: 10 min below the Torre del Time by the right fork of the Camino La Traviesa carry straight on to a poorly defined incut in the top of the ridge. Here go right (keeping left) down along the main path marked by cairns. This leads in 30 minutes (continually bearing left) to a house (large water pipe) – here either bear left along the defile-like camino on down towards the valley (¾ hr to the main road in La Punta) or straight on down along the track, which soon joins an unsurfaced road. To the left the route to the Mirador El Time continues (bus stop for bus 5, →Walk 50). To continue on down to La Punta, keep to the right on the track after 30m, before it goes down left again along water pipes – altogether it takes 1½ hrs from the Torre del Time to the main road in La Punta, 540m (bus stop for bus 11, 4km south of El Jesús).

The Torre del Time is often shrouded in clouds.

In late winter (almond blossom) and in spring (rock roses, broom flowers) this walk has a delightful display of flowers. The high point, however, is the splendid view from the look out plateau of the Torre del Time down into the depths of the Barranco de las Angustias, and towards the Caldera and the Aridane valley.

Between the **bus shelter** and the holy shrine a concreted track leads off which becomes a paved path and soon joins a road. Follow this for a good 15 minutes uphill until it passes a stone hut with barred gate and windows built in the hillside to the left of the road in a right-hand bend. Immediately after in the next left-hand bend a rather overgrown path goes off left (next to bundled water pipes). Immediately this becomes a beautiful paved path, which climbs up onto the top of the ridge. The path follows neglected terraced gardens with almond trees, fig cacti and medlar trees. After a good 10 minutes (track towards the end) the road is met again next to the school-house. Opposite, the old camino continues along the wall of the houses. This is followed straight on uphill (do not turn off left onto the track on the way) and after a good 10 minutes the road is joined again. Now follow the road for 20m uphill and turn off left onto the camino, which goes up to the

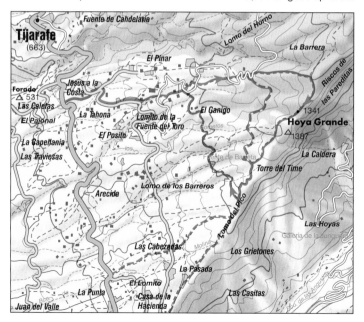

left (sign: Camino La Travesia). After just 5 minutes leave the camino to the right onto the road and continue on up opposite on the camino, which is at first cemented and then paved. Gradually the last houses from **El Pinar**, 1000m, are left behind, and after a good 10 minutes a forestry road is crossed. The path climbs up steeply through open pine forest and rock roses, crosses the forestry road another five times (keeping somewhat to the left on the last time; the forest road leads to the right in ½ hr directly to the Torre del Time) and goes up the ridge in a direct line (always follow the main path, cairns). Shortly before the crest of the ridge the path forks: here steeply straight on (left) upwards. About an hour after the last houses the crest of the ridge, 1500m, is reached. Here go to the right onto the path (sign) Roque de los Muchachos – Torre del Time. This leads down on the other side of the ridge through the slopes of the **Hoya Grande,** which are covered in broom, rock roses and pine forest, 1386m (sign after a good 10 minutes). Later the path leads to the left through terraced vineyards and half an hour after the crest of the ridge meets a track, from which a prominent path leads off to the right immediately after a turning to the left. This cuts off the bends in the track. Cross the track once, and the second time where there is a sign uphill to »Roque de los Muchachos« go left again towards the track (to the right is the shortest route back to El Jesús) and arrive shortly after at the fire watchtower, the **Torre del Time**, 1160m.

Past the tower, follow the track, which leads downhill for a good 5 minutes, until in a right-hand bend a wide path with stone walls goes off straight downhill. It leads over to the left in the direction of the crest of the ridge and after a good 5 minutes it forks. Here it is time for a decision: in order to go on to the Torre del Time or descend to La Punta, go straight on to the crest of the ridge (→Alternative), but to follow the main walk take the Camino La Travesia which leads off to the right and goes slightly up and down through the open pine forest. After a good 5 minutes stay on the straight path (path on right to »Sabina Canaria«, an old juniper tree). This contours beautifully across the hillside. After 20 minutes the path becomes a track, which then forks. Keep to the right and 5 minutes later go off left onto a narrow camino just before a right-hand bend in the track. This leads down rightwards into a barranco, which it immediately crosses, and after a short descent, climbs up the other side to a ridge. It then continues on across the hillside (not forking off down to the left). Afterwards the path goes across two further barrancos (a bit overgrown towards the end) and then goes up the hill (finally keeping right) to a couple of houses to meet a well next to a field path (sign). In a good 5 minutes this leads to the road in **El Pinar**. Now either go down along the road (4km) or go down left along the ascent path to **El Jesús**.

A beautiful camino leads between overgrown gardens down to La Punta.

27 From Puerto de Tazacorte to the Mirador El Time, 510m

Between heaven and earth – through the rock walls of the Angustias Gorge

Puerto de Tazacorte – Mirador El Time and back

Starting point: Puerto de Tazacorte, 10m (bus stop for bus 2) beach shop »Kiosco Teneguía« at the foot of the cliffs.
Walking time: Ascent good 1 hr, return route ¾ hr; total time 2 hrs
Ascent: Good 500m.
Grade: Easy walking, but a head for heights is a pre-requisite.
Refreshment: Bars and restaurants (fish!) in Puerto de Tazacorte, bar-restaurant at the Mirador El Time.
Combination possible with Walk 28.

Hardly any visitor to La Palma will leave out a visit to this fishing village: apart from the prized fish restaurants and the partly sandy beach, there is the spectacular situation of Puerto de Tazacorte at the end of the Barranco de las Angustias. Looking at the roughly 250m high cliffs at the back of the town hardly anybody would imagine that a footpath leads through them.

Immediately to the right next to the **Kiosco Teneguía** there is a small path leading off to the lower cliffs of the Angustias Gorge, which are peppered with caves. Keep to the right through rubbish and along banana plantations to the beginning of the Camino Real, which leads uphill in zigzags. Paths repeatedly lead off to the caves to the side of the camino, but ignore these and stick to the main path. For a good half hour the path »hangs« above the surging ocean, with Puerto de Tazacorte deep below, opposite Tazacorte and the Aridane Valley. Then just past where the paved path joins the end of a road at a viewing plateau. After a warehouse the paved path continues on the right. Shortly after it ends in another road, which is now followed up to the right past a number of villas with extravagantly lush gar-

On the Puerto de Tazacorte beach – in the background is the mighty wall of the Barranco de las Angustias through which the walk wends its way.

dens. A few minutes later at two reservoirs (left from the road) turn to the right onto a track which leads in between banana plantations. After about 5 minutes, shortly after a small stepped wall go right to a track. About 100m short of the drop into the Angustias Gorge it goes up left, changing to a tarmac road almost immediately, and leading in a quarter of an hour up to the **Mirador El Time** (bus stop for bus 5).

28 From Los Llanos to Puerto de Tazacorte

Through the Angustias Gorge to the Tazacorte Beach

Los Llanos – Barranco de las Angustias – Puerto de Tazacorte

Starting point: Los Llanos de Aridane bus station, 344m (buses 1-5).
Destination: Puerto de Tazacorte, 10m (bus stop for number 2 bus to Los Llanos).
Walking time: Los Llanos – Puerto de Tazacorte 1¼ hrs (1½ hrs in reverse direction).

Ascent: Just 350m.
Grade: Mainly easy walking along roads and paved paths, but nevertheless some unpleasant sections.
Refreshment: Bars and restaurants in Los Llanos and Puerto de Tazacorte.
Combination possible with Walk 27.

In the age of the car and intensive agriculture all too many of the old connecting paths between the different villages of the island have become disused or fallen victim to roads and plantations. This is also the case for the splendid Camino Real which leads from Los Llanos to Puerto de Tazacorte: only the upper section is still intact, the lower part is either derelict or interrupted by main roads.

From the bus station (Estacion de Autobuses) in **Los Llanos** go in the direction of the main road, but turn off before in the first street on the right – the wide Avenida Enrique Mederos, which leads largely parallel to the high street. Follow this to its end at the drop into the Angustias Gorge. Here go left onto a tarmac road. Keep right at the next crossing and then go right again after 100m onto the tarmac-surfaced Camino Punta de Argual (road sign; 20 minutes to this point). After a few minutes there is a right-hand

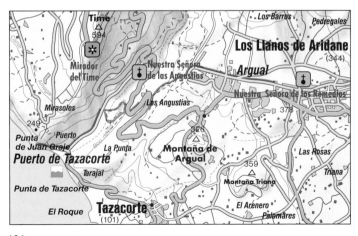

During the descent to the Barranco de las Angustias there is a splendid view towards the Caldera de Taburiente. The last houses in Los Llanos are in the right of the picture.

bend. 30m after this go left along the paved Camino Las Angustias down into the **Barranco de las Angustias**, with a splendid view of a large part of the gorge from the Caldera de Taburiente as far as Puerto de Tazacorte. Stay on the paved path, which joins the main road from Los Llanos to Puntagorda after a quarter of an hour. In order to avoid the continuation along the busy road as much as possible, one can continue on a path opposite; otherwise follow the road down. Already in the next sharp right-hand bend a little path goes off to the left where it is necessary to go down for five, steep and unpleasant metres under a large pipe. After this it is easy going again along a paved path, which is somewhat overgrown in parts. This leads down (keeping to the right towards the end) along the steep bank of the streambed to a banana plantation at a paled gate (15 minutes). To avoid the unpleasant section under the pipe continue along the main road to the next bend, where a good track leads off into the banana plantation. This leads along towards the left to also reach the gate to the banana plantation, which is always open. 10m from the gate there is a place where it is possible to descend into the bottom of the barranco. Now continue to **Puerto de Tazacorte** either in the bed of the stream or along the path next to the road past an estate of subsidised housing.

The South and the Cumbres

Cumbre Nueva and Cumbre Vieja – Rainforest and Volcanoes

Tourist attraction: Camels on the Volcán Antonio at Fuencaliente (Los Canarios).

Laurel forests on the Cumbre Nueva and open pine forests, wide black sandy landscapes, wild lava fields and elegantly-proportioned volcano cones on the Cumbre Vieja: these are the characteristic landscapes in the southern part of the island. With the exception of the densely wooded Cumbre Nueva, through which the »Túnel Grande« connects the eastern and western halves of the island, the vegetation tends to be sparse. Only succulents can manage on the dry lava ground, along with the canary island palm, laburnum and broom above 700m.

The south of La Palma is of more recent volcanic origin than the north. The 14km mountain chain of the Cumbre Vieja, which stretches from the Refugio El Pilar to the south tip on the Punta de Fuencaliente, consists of no less than 120 volcanoes. Perhaps the most beautiful of all the walks on the island, the Ruta de Volcanes, runs along the crest of the ridge. This walk not only takes in the highest point (Deseada, 1949m) but also the most significant craters (Hoyo Negro, Durazneros) of this impressive mountain range. Mighty lava streams spill down to the sea from the volcanoes and crater fissures of the Cumbre Vieja– the greatest of these is from the frozen lava stream, which erupted from San Juan in 1949 and flowed via *Las Manchas* to the sea near Puerto Naos. Further to the south past the flower village of *Jedey* there are repeated splendid views of the precipitous west coast, on which the most beautiful beaches of the island are found – one of the most well-known apart from the Puerto Naos being the Playa de Zamora at Las Indias. Then *Fuencaliente (Los Canarios)*: the most southerly town of the island attracts not only through the neat appearance of the town but through its picturesque situation between the gentle pine-covered slopes of the Cumbre Vieja and the wide lava surfaces of the San Antonio and Teneguía (eruption in 1971) volcanoes. It is moreover, known for its excellent wine, the »Teneguía« which can be tasted in the Bodegas of Teneguía. On the southern tip with the two lighthouses and the salt works there are, by the way, two fine beaches, the Playa del Faro and the Playa Nueva. Somewhat off the beaten track, but also beautiful, are the small beaches Playa del Río and Playa Martín, which can be reached via a 9km long unsurfaced road from *Montes de Luna*.

STARTING PLACES FOR WALKS

Centro de Visitantes de El Paso, 870m

National Park Visitor Centre on the main road from Los Llanos to Santa Cruz (bus stop for bus 1, at the turning off to Cumbrecita, 3.5km above the town centre of El Paso). Next to it is the Casa Forestall El Paso, opposite the Bar-restaurant Las Piedras.

Ermita de la Virgen del Pino, 900m

Small church in a beautiful position at the west foot of the Cumbre Vieja, 2km from the Centro de Visitantes, (signposted: first in the direction of Cumbrecita, then off to the right; nearest bus stop for bus 1 at the Centro de Visitantes, from there ½ hr on foot along the road).

Reventón, 1435m

Bumpy track along the ridge top of Cumbre Nueva (as far as Reventón Pass). Turn off at the Refugio El Pilar.

Refugio El Pilar, 1440m

Large picnic place with locked refuge hut, tables, benches and barbecue places on the vertex of the road from San Isidro (10km) – El Paso (12.5km). No bus connection. On foot best reached from:

■ Entrance to the tunnel on the road from Santa Cruz to Los Llanos (bus stop before the tunnel = »antes del tunél grande«); from here along an even forestry track through a laurel forest to the picnic site, Pared Vieja (sign, 1¾ hrs); from there along forest path and shortly after along the beautiful camino real to the right of the San Isidro – El Pilar road up to the height of the pass and the picnic place (¾ hr).

■ Left turn from the road to the Refugio El Pilar shortly after the base tunnel on the main road from Santa Cruz to Los Llanos (bus stop after the tunnel = »para del tunél grande«); keep going straight along the road to the picnic place (some short cuts possible, 1½ hrs).

■ Right-turn from a street at the upper end of the town of El Paso on the main road from Los Llanos to Santa Cruz (bus stop »Fuente Montaña Colorado«, good 5 minutes below the Centro de Visitantes); first along a road, later along camino to the dune landscape of Llano del Jable and along the road to the picnic area (2 hrs).

29 From El Paso to Breña Alta

Crossing of the Cumbre Nueva along an old connecting path

Centro de Visitantes de El Paso – Ermita de la Virgen del Pino – Reventón Pass – San Pedro de Breña Alta (– Santa Cruz)

Starting point: Centro de Visitantes de El Paso, 870m (bus stop for number 1 bus), at the upper end of the town of El Paso, 664m. Or Ermita de la Virgen del Pino, 900m.

Destination: San Pedro de Breña Alta, 344m (bus stop for buses 1, 6, 14).

Walking time: Centro de Visitantes – Ermita Virgen del Pino ½ hr, Ermita Virgen del Pino – Reventón Pass good 1 hr, Reventón Pass – Carretera de la Cumbre good 1¼ hrs, Carretera de la Cumbre – San Pedro 50 min; total time 4 hrs (return route 4½ hrs).

Ascent: 550m of ascent and nearly 1100m of descent.

Grade: Easy walking, although steep in places, on good caminos (slippery in wet!).

Refreshment: Bars/restaurants in San Pedro.

Alternative: From San Pedro de Breña Alta to Mirador de la Concepción: From the Plaza go on along the main street and take the first right (Calle El Arco) down to the parish church. Go left next to the church into the Calle Blas Perez Gonzalez. The road is later called Camino Real and runs parallel to the main road, after 10 min next to it on the right. 5 min later it crosses a road and becomes a path, which a few minutes later at a crossing (bar) joins the Carretera de la Cumbre. Now continue opposite along the road and 50m later up the road to the right to the Mirador de la Concepción (½ hr from San Pedro; possible descent to Santa Cruz, →Walk 2)

Combinations possibility with Walks 5, 6, 30, 42.

The Camino real over the Reventón Pass was once the most important connecting path between the Aridane Valley and Santa Cruz. It is exceptionally well constructed and runs over the east side of the Cumbre Nueva through splendid laurel forest.

At the start there is a half hour trip along roads. Turn off next to the **Centro de Visitantes** onto the road in the direction of Cumbrecita and go right at the crossing after nearly 15 minutes to the **Ermita Virgen del Pino**. Immediately behind the beautifully situated chapel a wide forestry track leads into the pine forest. It goes straight up the weakly

The Ermita de la Virgen del Pino at the foot of the Cumbre Vieja.

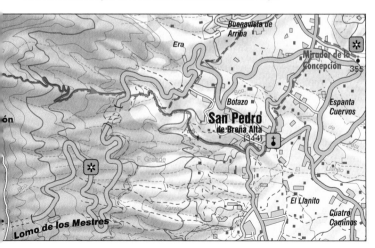

In the Barranco de Laja – view back to the Cumbre Nueva.

defined ridge. After a good quarter of an hour the foot of the escarpment is reached. Here the paved Camino Real begins. This leads up in zigzags along a fire break and brings fine views of the Aridane Valley and the Cumbrecita with its surroundings., The path, which is rather steep in parts, can be very slippery if wet. The scrub contains rock roses, ferns, tree heaths and laurel shrubs, and the pines with their »Xmas tree decoration« of hanging moss are particularly fascinating. After a drawn out traverse rightwards across the hillside and a left-hand bend, the crest of the Cumbre Nueva (**Reventón Pass**, 1410m) is finally reached at a point where an unsurfaced road is crossed.

The track forks to the left. Stay right here and go immediately right onto the camino, which leads off down the east side of the Cumbre. Initially it leads slightly up and down across the hillside and then drops in wide bends down through the rainforest. After a good half hour a forestry track is reached, which is followed down to the right. A few minutes later straight after the first left-hand bend the old paved path branches off sharply to the right to end shortly after in a forestry track, which leads easily on downwards. It is only after another 10 minutes after four loops in the path that the old path goes off sharply to the left again. It soon joins up with a track and shortly after passes a rest place with a stone bench. About 15 minutes later there is another stone bench. 5 minutes after this a covered canal crosses the path, the Canal de Fuencaliente (→Walk 5) and after another 5 minutes the main road is reached (**Carretera de la Cumbre**).

Follow the main road for about 50m to the left until the camino continues downwards along a stone wall on the right. After a good 10 minutes it crosses an unsurfaced road (go on down diagonally leftwards) and soon afterwards passes a solitary house. Shortly after it crosses the Barranco de Laja and goes along the left side of the valley. After a good 50m in front of a chestnut tree a camino bordered by stone walls leads off sharply to the right (the main path straight on leads up to the main road). It curves back to the bed of the stream and leads steadily downhill along this. A canal is crossed after 5 minutes and a few minutes later at the first houses the path becomes a tarmac road. This is followed straight on downwards and after 10 minutes the main road from Breña Alta to Mazo (not through the underpass) leads leftwards in just 5 minutes to the Plaza of **San Pedro de Breña Alta**. From here it is possible to continue walking to the Mirador de la Concepción and Santa Cruz (→Alternative).

End of the walk: the Plaza of San Pedro de Breña Alta.

30 Over the Cumbre Nueva

Panoramic circuit along royal paths and good tracks

Ermita de la Virgen del Pino – Reventón – Refugio El Pilar – Llano del Jable – Centro de Visitantes de El Paso – Ermita de la Virgen del Pino

Location: El Paso, 664m.
Starting point: Ermita de la Virgen del Pino, 900m. If arriving by bus the walk starts from the Centro de Visitantes de El Paso (bus stop for number 1 bus).
Walking time: Ermita Virgen del Pino – Reventón Pass good 1 hr, Reventón Pass – Refugio El Pilar 1½ hrs, Refugio El Pilar – Centro de Visitantes 1¾ hrs, Centro de

Visitantes – Ermita Virgen del Pino ½ hr; total time 5 hrs.
Ascent: About 650m.
Grade: Easy overall, but long.
Refreshment: Bar-restaurant Las Piedras opposite the Centro de Visitantes de El Paso.
Combination possible with Walks 6, 29, 31, 32, 33, 42.

The ascent along the Camino real (royal way) to Reventón would be a good walk in its own right, with the laurel forest and the views of the Aridane Valley and of the east coast, from the top. This would offer the walker enough amusement for an easy half-day. Nevertheless, despite some monotonous stretches of track and road, the descent via the Refugio El Pilar can be recommended for its lava flows and volcanic ash fields, which offer a glimpse of the more recent geological history of the island.

From the **Ermita del Virgen del Pino** follow →Walk 29 to the **Reventón Pass**, 1416m. Here go right onto the unsurfaced road (sign: »Refugio El Pilar«, white and red markings). This leads over the top of the ridge of the Cumbre Nueva to the Refugio El Pilar and luckily sees little traffic. Only rarely can the Aridane Valley in the west and Santa Cruz in the east, not to mention the trade wind clouds, which frequently shroud the ridge, be glimpsed through the jungle of laurel trees, rock roses and ferns. After 30 minutes **Reventón** (Cumbrera), 1435m, with its radio masts is passed. Shortly after at the small car park with the sign on the rock »Fuente a 200m« a detour can be made on the left along a steep path, slippery in places, to an enclosed spring in the laurel forest (15 min, one way). A good half hour later a track crosses the pista, but this is not taken. The somewhat monotonous but altogether very gentle walk along the ridge soon comes to an end. In front is the mighty elegantly proportioned volcanic core of Pico Birigoyo, and the road from San Isidro to El Paso is reached. (Immediately before the junction a beautiful camino real goes off to the left to the Pared Vieja picnic area: →Walk 6). In a few minutes the road leads right to the **Refugio El Pilar** picnic area, 1440m. – Now follow →Walk 6 to the **Centro de Visitantes** de El Paso. Here turn off to the left on the road towards Cumbrecita. From here it is only 15 minutes to the point where the approach road to **Ermita Virgen del Pino** forks off to the right.

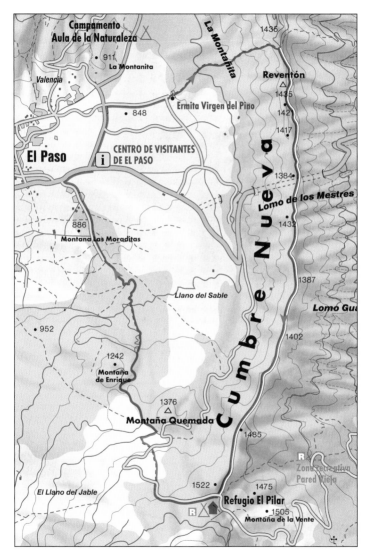

31 From El Paso to Volcán San Juan, 1300m

To the crater fissure of the most impressive lava stream on the island

Tacande de Arriba (El Paso) – Llano del Jable – Volcán San Juan – Hoyo de la Sima – Jedey

Starting point: Kilometre sign »km 1« in Tacande de Arriba, 680m, on the road from El Paso – San Nicolás/Las Manchas (no bus connection; nearest bus stop for bus 1 in El Paso, 1km).

Destination: Jedey, 620m (bus stop for bus 3), 6km south of Tacande.

Walking time: Tacande de Arriba – El Llano del Jable 1¾ hrs, El Llano del Jable – Volcán San Juan ¾ hr, Volcán San Juan – Hoyo de la Sima good ¾ hr, Hoyo de la Sima – Jedey 1½ hrs; total time 5 hrs.

Ascent: 650m of ascent and 700m of descent.

Grade: Mainly easy walking, but long (mainly forestry roads).

Refreshment: Only in El Paso or in Jedey/San Nicolás (Bodega Tamanca).

Alternative: The following way back can be recommended if a circuit is preferred (very worthwhile, but a good sense of direction is necessary as the line of the walk is difficult to see in places). From the turning area go down for nearly half an hour along the steep, slippery path on the left bank of the San Juan lava stream until an obvious fork is reached. Here go to the right down through the lava stream and in a bend go through the roughly 5-metre wide lava channel (on the left in the continuation of the channel there is an impressive lava tunnel). 20 metres after continue sharply right and go up slightly to the left to the other bank of the lava stream, on the edge of which the path continues to ascend (fine view of Volcán San Juan). After a few minutes at the last tongue of lava the path turns away from the lava stream and leads gently up and down through the open pine forest. A few minutes later the path becomes a track, which is followed straight on. After 20 minutes at a small valley with chestnut trees next to a small house the track forks. Here go left along the gently downward leading track, which soon ends in an unsurfaced road, which crosses it. Straight on there is a path, which is difficult to see. It leads to the right, at first gently downwards and then slightly up and down across the sandy hillside (for orientation: after 10 minutes, the path, which is now clearly visible, passes 5m above a large, regular-shaped hollow); ignore paths going off to the left or right. After a traverse of about 30 minutes the wide camino real bordered by stone walls and familiar from the ascent is reached. If this is followed down to the turning area for 25 minutes, the tarmac road is reached, which leads back to Tacande de Arriba in a further 25 minutes (2¾ hrs in total from the turning area). By the way: For anyone who is not keen to follow the steep, slippery path along the lava stream, it is also possible to continue walking along the forestry road in the direction of Hoyo de la Sima and after about 40 min (10 min after a left-hand loop) to take a forestry road which goes off sharply to the right. Follow this straight on to its end in front of two small barranco channels, which lead down parallel to each other (to the left between the two channels, there is a possible descent to the nearby forestry road, which leads on down to Jedey). Here go straight on along the path, which leads down between the right-hand barranco channel and a mighty lava wall of San Juan. Shortly after it joins up with the path leading down from the turning area (½ hr longer).

Combination possible with Walk 30.

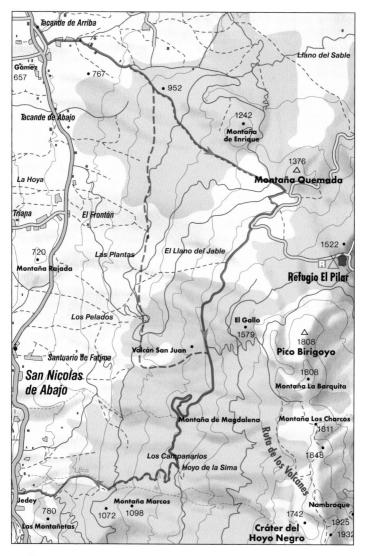

The goal of this walk is San Juan, which in 1949 sent out a mighty lava stream towards the west coast burying large areas in the region of San Nicolás and Las Manchas. Equally interesting is the mighty volcano crack of Hoyo de la Sima which is also touched upon by this long walk through thoroughly charming landscapes. To cut the walk down to 3 hours and thereby avoid the rather steep and bumpy ascent from Tacande, it is possible to begin on the road from El Paso to Refugio El Pilar (forestry track turning off to Fuencaliente).

At the kilometre sign »km 1« at the beginning of **Tacande de Arriba**, leave the country road for the narrow uphill-leading tarmac road and then go left at the first large turning off into the Calle Cuesta de Juliana. After half an hour, well past the last houses in Tacande, the tarmac ends. Straight on (not left) there is a dilapidated Camino Real bordered by stonewalls. The stony path leads up quite steeply through the pine forest and after an hour of walking it reaches a small rise with a view of the Montaña de Enrique. Half an hour later it joins a forestry road, which is followed straight on upwards. After a quarter of an hour the **Llano de Jable** is reached, a wide, pitch-black sand plateau at the foot of the Pico Birigoyo. Continue straight on and go up over the sand slopes to the tarmac road in the direction of the Refugio El Pilar. This is followed to the right to the first sharp left-hand bend (small parking area and lookout point). A sand track goes off to the right from here in the direction of Fuencaliente after a good half hour leading past a turning area above the **Volcán San Juan** lava stream. Whoever wants to can descend in a few minutes via a steep but obvious path to the eruption point of San Juan – no crater, indeed nothing at all that would remind one of a vol-

Tubo in the San Juan lava stream.

cano; only a crack in the ground, from which a ditch, at first small, but then wider and wider, leads off in the direction of Puerto Naos. It is a black, wildly rearing lava ribbon, which has mercilessly laid itself over the cultivated land at the foot of the Cumbre Vieja.

It is now possible to return to Tacande de Arriba either via the familiar route (2hrs) or along the →alternative (2¾ hrs; impressive views of the San Juan lava stream). The suggested walk, however, descends to Jedey and so continues along the wide forestry road (two hairpin bends en route). After three-quarters of an hour a forestry road

The San Juan lava stream with the Cumbre Vieja, seen from San Nicolás.

goes off right to Jedey (sign): ignore this. 5 minutes later the forestry road leads past the fenced off hole in the ground of **Hoyo de Sima**, about 1200m. Immediately afterwards another forestry road goes off to the right to Jedey (sign). Keep going down this, always along the main track. Further down this joins up with the other forestry road and offers splendid views of the west coast, and later on into the Barranco de las Palmas with its lava flows and then of the volcanic chimney of Montaña Marcos. After 1½ hrs the good track – tarmac for the last section, reaches the main road in **Jedey**. The bus stop is on the right next to Bar Jedey.

32 Pico Birigoyo, 1808m

Fine panoramic summit suitable for less serious walkers

Refugio El Pilar – Pico Birigoyo – Refugio El Pilar

Location: El Paso, 664m (bus stop for bus 1).
Starting point: Refugio El Pilar, 1440m (no bus connection).
Walking time: Ascent 1¼ hrs, descent ¾ hr; total time 2 hrs.
Ascent: Almost 400m.
Grade: Easy, not very strenuous walk. The summit ridge is dangerous in storm conditions.
Combination possible with Walks 6, 30 and 33.

Anyone who experiences this splendid volcano core on a cloudless day is lucky: it is then possible to look down on the black lava surfaces, which lead down in the direction of El Paso. The views of the Aridane Valley and the west coast are also fantastic. Opposite – near enough to touch – is the Caldera summit and in the south are the volcanoes as far as Deseada. Few of La Palma's summits can match these views. The beige-coloured volcanic cone, which can be clearly seen from far off, can of course be »picked off« on the »Ruta de los Volcanes«, but it doesn't deserve such treatment: it would be a shame to just make a quick detour to it. So allow several hours time and enjoy the unique panorama.

View from the Birigoyo summit to the Caldera de Taburiente.

The perfectly formed volcanic core of Pico Birigoyo, seen here from the road near the Refugio El Pilar.

To start with the walk is the same as the Ruta de los Volcanes: immediately behind the **El Pilar** refuge hut is a low building from which a clear red and white marked path leads up the hill, keeping to the right. Stay on the main path, which goes around Birigoyo to the west i.e. keeping right at the fork after 10 minutes. 5 minutes later a small viewing platform is passed with a splendid view of El Paso and the Caldera surroundings. The pine forest now becomes increasingly open and the path contours the volcanic ash flank of a subsidiary summit of Birigoyo. After a total of 40 minutes the path ends in a forestry road. Follow this to the left for only about 5 minutes, until a more or less clear path marked with cairns goes off uphill to the left. A small depression is reached shortly afterwards. From here keep to the left (a path comes from the right), up to the next rise on the edge of the crater opposite Birigoyo. After a short walk on the right edge of the crater the triangulation pillar on **Pico Birigoyo** is reached. The descent is best done over the ridge, which leads to the northeast in the direction of the starting point. So from the triangulation pillar go down the obvious path on scree to the foot of the tree-covered depression below the summit. This is followed by a short traverse of the hillside to the right into the pine forest, from which a wide tree-free break leads down to the San Isidro – El Pilar road. Immediately after a reservoir a white-yellow waymarked path crosses the break. This leads in 5 minutes through the pine forest back to the **Refugio El Pilar** (it is also possible to continue going down the break to the road and to then go back left along this to the picnic area).

33 Ruta de los Volcanes

The Volcano Route – the showpiece walk of the island

Refugio El Pilar – Cráter del Hoyo Negro (– Nambroque) – Deseada II – Volcán Martín – Fuencaliente

Starting point: Refugio El Pilar, 1440m (no bus connection).

Destination: Fuencaliente (Los Canarios), 722m (bus stop for bus 3).

Walking time: Refugio El Pilar – Deseada II 3¼ hrs, Deseada II – Fuencaliente 3¼ hrs; total time 6½ hrs (in opposite direction: Fuencaliente – Deseada II 4½ hrs, Deseada II – El Pilar 2¾ hrs).

Ascent: Ascent to Deseada 500m, descent to Fuencaliente 1250m.

Grade: Strenuous mountain walk requiring fitness and sure-footedness. Along the crest of the ridge there is often low cloud and extremely stormy winds which can force one to turn back.

Refreshment: Various bars/restaurants and bodegas in Fuencaliente.

Alternatives: The volcano route can be split into two sections: Refugio El Pilar – Deseada and Fuencaliente – Deseada. From the col between V. Martín and Los Faros fit walkers can return by descending keeping slightly right, going past Montaña Pelada on the right to a forestry road (good ½ hr, →Walk 34) and along this to the right in about 4 hrs to the Refugio El Pilar (total time 9–10 hrs).

Combination possible with Walks 32, 34 and 35.

Tranquil start: view of the upper Aridane Valley.

Ascent to the crest of the Cumbre Vieja.

The traverse of the Cumbre Vieja is one of the greatest and most breathtaking walks on the island – not only because of the continually varied landscape and the insight it provides into the volcanic history of the »isla bonita« but also because of the tremendous views of the west and east coasts. Nevertheless, whoever wishes to attempt the route should not overlook the fact that it is a strenuous day's walk. Moreover, sudden, unexpected bad weather conditions with cloud, fog and a strong to hurricane force wind can occur on the crest of the ridge.

The red and white markings of the Ruta de los Volcanes begin immediately to the right of the **Refugio El Pilar**. To begin with the path leads through splendid pine forest; later the view of the mountain surroundings of the Caldera de Taburiente and the Aridane Valley opens up. Now cross the volcanic ash flank of Birigoyo – only ferns, broom bushes and pine shoots brighten the landscape which is dominated by black sand. After 40 minutes the path joins a forestry road, which is followed uphill to the left. 15 minutes later – once again in an open pine forest – a path off to the right, at first bordered by stone walls, goes around to the west of the next volcanic cones. The landscape which follows, which is naturally almost like a park, is amongst the most beautiful that La Palma has to offer: broom bushes nestle in the ochre-coloured volcanic ash, light-green pine shoots contrast with the dark lava scree and pine groves cover the path with a soft carpet of needles. Deep below is the west coast with its green banana plantations and the house roofs. A small wooden bridge is crossed and then an ascent is made up a shimmering red and yellow coloured erosion ditch to the crest and along this to the highest point of the ridge (1904m). Behind is a view of Santa Cruz and Los Llanos. Then go on down along the edge of the deeply incut, strongly eroded basin of the **Cráter del Hoyo Negro**. The path now keeps to the left and avoids the next rise on the left. Here a detour to **Nambroque**, 1924m, which drops away steeply to the east, is worthwhile (¼ hr): an imposing panoramic summit with a number of dikes, small craters and an unfathomably deep hole under the ground on the edge of the path before the saddle.

Further along the volcano route the next volcanic basin with the pitch-black lava field of La Malforada is visible. The path goes along to the right along the crater and forks at the lowest point of the edge of the crater at the foot of the Montaña del Fraile. Straight on a path goes off to the main summit of Deseada, 1945m (the path may be closed off; en route it skirts the Cráter del Duraznero, here go left) – for this walk, however, stay to the right along the marked main path. First it leads gently downwards in a wide curve around Duraznero and goes through an increasingly steep valley up to the summit of **Deseada II**,

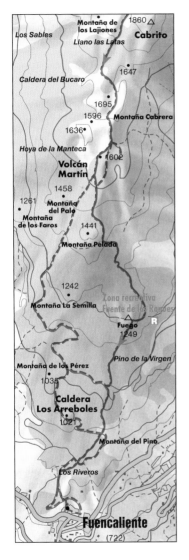

1932m. A splendid panorama is the reward, and besides the Caldera frame and distant parts of the Volcano Route, it also includes a splendid view of the west coast; from the main summit (10 min) the east coast can also be seen. In the distance Gomera, Tenerife and Hierro are visible.

Continue southwards along the top of the ridge to the gentle summits of Montaña los Bermejales and Montaña de los Lajiones, in which a small dark rock wall has crept in. Keeping slightly to the left there is a short section through a pine wood. The path then goes uphill a little and on through a flat dip to the east of Montaña de los Lajiones. There is then a long drawn out little valley, which leads between several rises – a rather flat but still beautiful terrain for scree glissading. Gradually more and more pines are found on the edge of the path. This is an idyllic spot especially when the laburnum is in flower. Soon the pines become less frequent: the path rising slightly goes to the left around a dark volcanic core (Caldera del Búcaro) and leads on to a weakly defined saddle (1638m). Now Volcán Martín is visible. Go along down the ridge to a fork shortly before the edge of the red-coloured Martín Crater (1552m). Straight on it is possible to make a detour to the summit of **Volcán Martín**, 1597m (possibly closed off), or to the Fuente del Fuego in the Martín Crater (10 minutes for either; see Walk 34). For the guidebook walk, however, stay to the right on the

High point: the Deseada summit.

main path, which leads across the scree-covered flank to a col between the volcano and the Faros summit. Now walk on over volcanic ash slopes directly towards the brownish double summit of **Montaña Pelada** (keep left at forks in the path) which the Volcano Route avoids to the left with fine views of the secondary crater situated to the south of Martín. 25 minutes from the saddle the path levels out in a pine forest and there is a fork immediately afterwards. The Volcano Route goes off to the left here and leads steeply down to the Martín lava flow, on the right edge of which it continues towards the valley. Soon a wider, more even path appears which is abandoned for another to the left after a few minutes. A few minutes later a camino is crossed (Sign: »Vereda de las Cabras«) and the path continues straight on in the direction of Fuente de los Roques. The path now continues ascending slightly through an undulating sand landscape to the foot of **Fuego** (Montaña la Semilla, 1248m), which is turned to the left. After 10 min-

The La Malforada lavafield with the Montaña del Fraile.

Leisurely end to the walk: the path from Volcán Martín (background) to Fuencaliente.

utes there is a steep track (which is ignored) off to the left to the nearby, picnic area of Fuente de los Roques, which is already visible. A few minutes later the path on the south side of the Fuego forks once again – here go left down along the obvious stone-bordered path. To the left, the destination of the next leg of the walk can be seen: the **Montaña del Pino,** 1039m (radio masts). A quarter of an hour later a forestry track is crossed at its north foot and the mountain is avoided to the right, immediately crossing another unsurfaced road. The track now drops down more steeply. Only after another quarter of an hour – another unsurfaced road is crossed – does it level out a bit again. The camino is now bordered by stone walls and passes the first vineyards. After 10 minutes of following the path straight on, another unsurfaced road is crossed. The path now skirts another mountain to the right and ends after a few minutes in an unsurfaced road. This is followed to the left and abandoned after 5 minutes for a track which bears off to the left (keep left again at the next fork after 50m). Now Fuencaliente, the end of the walk, can be seen below. After a few minutes the unsurfaced road is crossed again keeping to the left, and then the church is reached, followed 100m after by the main road of **Fuencaliente** (Los Canarios).

34 Volcán Martín, 1597m

Sandy slopes and an impressive crater cave

Fuencaliente – Volcán Martín – Montaña Pelada – Fuencaliente

Location: Fuencaliente (Los Canarios), 722m (bus stop for bus 3).

Starting point: From the church square above the main road, go right and then up the first road to the left (tarmac for a short distance, then a bumpy unsurfaced road). After 0.7km – sportsground on the left – continue to the right. After 1.5km there is a sign on a tree: »M.U.P. Fuencaliente/Llano de los Cestos«: go right here, passing a concrete silo after 600m, still uphill on the unsurfaced road. After 2.5km, same sign again – go left. After 4.8km there is a level clearing – »Llano de los Cestos« – carry straight on. Go right after 6.7km. After 7.2km there is a large track fork, 1180m – the starting point of the walk, where there is a sign on a tree »Ruta de los Vulcánes« (1¾ hrs on foot from Fuencaliente).

Walking time: Ascent 1¼ hrs (cave an additional 20min), return path 1 hr; total time 2¼ hrs (5¼ hrs from Fuencaliente).

Ascent: Good 400m.

Grade: Easy mountain walking although a bit strenuous on the ascent.

Refreshment: Various bars, restaurants and bodegas in Fuencaliente.

Combination possible with Walks 33, 35.

Advice: It is possible that the summit ridge of Volcán Martín is closed (conservation).

Splendid landscape of sand and a phenomenal view towards the south peak are the highlights of this walk on Volcán Martín.

Directly on the track crossing there is a path marked by cairns which goes off uphill to the Ruta de los Volcanes (sign). After a few minutes an unsurfaced road is crossed (sign: »Fuente del Tíon«). Continue straight on along the stone-bordered path; there are young pines and laburnum bushes along the way and Montaña Pelada rises up on the right hand side.

The cave with a spring in the ruggedly romantic crater of Volcán Martín.

After a good half hour a small rise is reached – a beautiful place in the middle of even sand hills. A slight dip follows, after which continue straight on keeping slightly to the right up the side of Martín in a col (20 min; now white-red markings) and onwards along a col on the north side of Martín (5 min). Here it is recommended to make a detour into the Martín Crater with the Fuente del Fuego: first go sharply right in the direction of the summit, then left along a path to the deepest point on the crater edge and then right over scree down into the crater: in the opposite wall is the cave in which the dripping water is collected in hollowed out tree trunks (10 min one-way). Back at the col again it is only 10 minutes along the narrow edge of the crater to reach the summit of **Volcán Martín**. From the summit a wide footpath leads down across the scree in a south-westerly direction to meet the white-red marked path after a few minutes (it is also possible to go back to the col and walk down the white-red marked Ruta de los Volcanes keeping left all the time). This leads leftwards over to **Montaña Pelada** (5 min) and avoids the volcano summit by going leftwards across the slope. After a few minutes the path enters an open pine forest and forks. Here go straight on, while the Ruta de los Volcanes goes off to the left. Afterwards keep on the path which crosses the slope (watch out for marking stones). After about 10 minutes it leads past a small rise (do not go up to the left here) and crosses a track. The path goes up and down slightly across the slope, parallel to a track, which is crossed after just 10 minutes. 100m later the crossing Fuente del Tíon – Ruta de los Volcanes is reached (sign). Continue along the approach route, which leads down to the left to the starting point.

35 From Montes de Luna to Fuego, 1248m

Enjoyable walk through a splendid lava landscape

Montes de Luna – Fuente de los Roques – Fuego – Montes de Luna

Starting point: Bus shelter / Bar Casa Augusto in Montes de Luna, 740m (bus stop for buses 3 and 7) on the main road from Mazo to Fuencaliente.
Walking time: Montes de Luna – Fuente los Roques good 1¾ hrs, Fuente de los Roques – Fuego ¼ hr, Fuego – Montes de Luna good 1½ hrs; total time 3¾ hrs.
Ascent: 600m in total.
Grade: Mainly easy walking along gener-

ally good tracks and forest roads.
Refreshment: Bars in Montes de Luna.
Combination possible with Walks 33 and 34.
Advice: The walk can also be started from the Fuente de los Roques picnic area (reached via a forestry road, which goes off from the Montes de Luna – Fuencaliente main road at about Km 25.5).

Montes de Luna and the Fuente de los Roques picnic area are ideal starting points for various expeditions through the splendid pine forests and volcanic landscapes on the south end of the Cumbre Vieja. The wonderful walk which ascends to Fuego from the picnic area touches on the impressive lava stream from Volcán Martín on the return route.

On the left of the Casa Augusto Bar on the main street in **Montes de Luna** a steep lane (Camino de Tira) leads upwards, joining a wide tarmac road after 5 minutes. Go left along this (the road immediately becomes narrower) and after 100m go onto a paved path, which goes up to the right (towards a white cross) and straight on across the slope. After about 10 minutes it crosses a forestry road (the later return route) and forks a few minutes later – here bear right slightly uphill. The camino crosses the mighty lava flow of Volcán Martín between a wooden cross and a stone pillar and then, after a total of 45 minutes becomes a forestry track. After 200m this joins an unsurfaced forestry road, which comes up from the main road and provides the continuation to the picnic area of

Fuente de los Roques. So follow the pista uphill to the right through the beautiful pine forest with its high trees, bearing sharply right at a fork after half an hour, (a forestry track leads off to Fuencaliente on the left). 5 minutes later leave the main track which veers off to the left for a forestry road which goes straight on in the direction of Fuente de los Roques (sign). This passes two beautiful volcanic vents, and after 20 minutes leads to a crossroad of tracks before the Volcán Martín lava flow. Here go left onto the forestry road that leads to the picnic area of **Fuente de los Roques**, 1220m, which is reached after 10 minutes. The beautiful picnic area situated at the foot of a group of crags has a play area, barbecue places, toilets and a spring (back to the right, at the foot of the crags).

Immediately after the entrance to the fenced off picnic area a path goes off to the right to Fuego (sign). This leads up steeply to a small col above the crags ending at the white-red waymarked Ruta de los Volcanes (→Walk 33). It is possible to continue straight on walking in the direction of Fuencaliente but our walk keeps sharply to the right and after 5 minutes of ascent reaches another fork with a view towards Montaña Pelada and to the beautifully shaped Volcán Martín. Here a detour is possible which leads upwards to the left along a narrow path reaching the trigonometry pillar on the crater edge of Fuego (Montaña la Semilla) after a few minutes: here a view opens out to Fuencaliente and Volcán San Antonio.

Back again at the last fork, follow the white-red waymarked path, which leads along a black sandy, pine-covered plateau directly to Volcán Martín. After 10 minutes a crossing of tracks is reached at the foot of Montaña Pelada. Here leave the Ruta de los Volcanes, which now climbs up to Volcán Martín (good ½ hr), and take the path which goes off to the right (sign: »Vereda de las Cabras«). This goes gently downwards and soon leads leftwards into the lava field of Volcán Martín – a really charming section of the walk. After 10 minutes, finally through a lava runnel, the other »bank« of the lava flow is reached, where the path branches again. Keep right here (straight on there is a beautiful path through the east flank of Volcán Martín) and follow the unclear path, which keeps left somewhat to the side of the lava flow, leading down in a good five minutes to the Fuencaliente – Mazo / El Pilar forestry road. (On the right there is a possible way back to the Fuente de los Roques picnic area, 20 min). Keep left along the road and after a few minutes turn off right onto a forestry road (barrier), which leads down through the pine forest in many bends – a leisurely descent on a soft pine carpet. After three-quarters of an hour the road meets at right angles with the camino, which is already familiar from the ascent, and this leads leftwards in a quarter of an hour back to **Montes de Luna**.

36 From Fuencaliente to Volcán Teneguía and the lighthouse on the south point

Sandy pleasure and hot earth – an insight into the most recent volcanic history of La Palma

Fuencaliente – Volcán San Antonio – Roque Teneguía – Volcán Teneguía – Faro de Fuencaliente – Fuencaliente

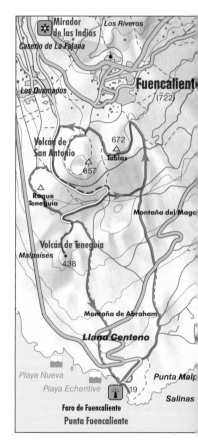

Location: Fuencaliente (Los Canarios), 722m (bus stop for bus 3).

Starting point: Paying car park at Volcán San Antonio, 630m. From the centre of Fuencaliente go along the road in the direction of Las Indias, turning left after the last houses along a signposted unsurfaced road to the nearby car park at the upper foot of Volcán San Antonio (about 15 min on foot).

Walking time: Detour to Volcán San Antonio 20 min, San Antonio – Teneguía car park 50 min, ascent/descent of Volcán Teneguía 35 min, return to San Antonio 1¼ hrs; total time 3 hrs. Alternative: Teneguía car park – Faro de Fuencaliente good 1 hr, Faro de Fuencaliente – San Antonio 2 hrs; total time then 5 hrs.

Ascent: Volcán Teneguía good 300m, Lighthouse extra 450m.

Grade: Generally easy walking but on the wind-exposed ridges of San Antonio and Teneguía it can be dangerous at times (frequent storm force winds); ascent to Teneguía requires sure-footedness. Don't forget bathing costumes (Playa del Faro).

Refreshment: Beach restaurant at Faro de Fuencaliente; various bars, restaurants and bodegas in Fuencaliente.

Advice: It is also possible to begin the walk from the car park at the foot of Volcán Teneguía or from the lighthouse.

The volcano walk on the crater of Volcán San Antonio and Volcán Teneguía offers an insight into the most recent volcanic history of the island; while the crater basin of the

View from the Teneguía summit to Volcán San Antonio.

exemplary volcanic cone of San Antonio has already been colonised by pine saplings, there is still a slight sulphur smell in the air on Teneguía, which erupted in 1971, and there are still a number of hot places on the surface of the ground.

From the car park at **Volcán San Antonio** first follow the crater path, which after a few metres leads to the crater edge of the long extinct volcano. The view stretches over large areas of the southern part of the island. After 10 minutes the point for turning back at the trigonometry pillar, 657m, is reached: the former path around the crater has been closed off on environmental grounds.

Back again at the car park, go off left along the signposted path to Volcán Teneguía. This leads downhill in steep zigzags and after a few minutes, crosses a covered canal. After a quarter of an hour of steep descent the path ends in an unsurfaced road, which is followed to the left. This leads easily across the slope and offers splendid views over vineyards towards the west coast. Soon **Roque Teneguía** is visible on the right and is reached by turning off after nearly a quarter of an hour along a wide path marked with rows of stones. This leads in wide loops down to the volcanic vent (good 5 minutes; don't turn off right along the way). On the rocks on the flat south side numerous prehistoric rock engravings can be seen (mainly spirals). The path leads to the left past Roque Teneguía then past a second volcanic vent and then dips down through a sandy runnel to a canal, which is followed to the left. This leads directly to Volcán Teneguía, passing a large res-

131

View downwards from Roque Teneguía.

ervoir after 10 minutes. Leave the canal at this point and follow the track below it, which in a few minutes leads to the foot of Teneguía where an unsurfaced road ends in a car park. The ascent of Teneguía takes the obvious path, which leads to the summit with its numerous eruption craters and the most varied, shimmering red and yellow colours. It winds along the narrow ridge on the edge of the crater (numerous hot spots on the edge of the path) and finally leads along a sharp ridge to the highest point of **Volcán Teneguía**, 438m. In a storm this is a dangerous adventure that is best avoided! From the summit the south point with its lighthouse can already be seen and in the distance Tenerife, La Gomera and El Hierro can be spotted.

Back at the car park it is necessary to decide. If the descent to the lighthouses is not intended then go up the unsurfaced approach road to the large fork. Here continue to the right along the road. At the fork on the mountain col after 5 minutes bear to the left. About 200m later a track crossroads is reached (from the right the ascent path from the lighthouse described below joins): here take the track on the left. This goes straight on, gradually steeper, up between vineyards. After half an hour a beautiful valley is reached, which is bordered on the right by a weathered volcanic vent. Soon after a crossroad of tracks is reached where one keeps left. The unsurfaced road goes up gently across the hillside and views of the South Point and Teneguía open out. Above on the rise, stay on the pista which soon, already with a view of Fuencaliente, winds over to the left to the car park at **Volcán San Antonio**.

Descent from Volcán Teneguía to Faro de Fuencaliente: About 50 m from the car park an obvious path branches off rightwards (east) from the Teneguía summit path. Immediately a path goes off left to a miniature crater, but walk straight on to the right along the main path, which is marked by

rows of stones. This crosses a lava field, then runs along its edge and after just a quarter of an hour it forks in the direction of the walk. Here bear right onto the narrower path, which continues through the lava field. After some minutes – the lava field has been left behind – the path bordered by stones dips more

The salt works and the lighthouse at the Punta de Fuencaliente.

steeply in the direction of the already visible lighthouse. After half an hour a road is reached. Follow this for 50 metres to the right to the next bend, in which the continuation of the path bears off to the left. A few minutes later it crosses the road again and then dips down fairly directly towards the lighthouse, crossing a road again after a quarter of an hour. The **Faro de Fuencaliente** is reached 5 minutes later. Behind the lighthouse which was erected in 1984, (next to it is an old lighthouse) blinding white salt works spread out, and to the right below them is the small beach: the Playa del Faro, on which a small beach restaurant (good fish) awaits a visit.

For the return route follow the approach road, turning right onto the unsurfaced road to Las Cabras in the large left-hand bend after 5 minutes. It leads up to a wind power station and splits after about 8 minutes at the level of the turbines. Here continue left, above a gravel works. Immediately afterwards red and white pillars appear on the side of the road indicating the continuing route. Shortly after, go left again at a fork in the road and 100 metres later follow the pillars to the left up across a volcanic ash slope. After 20 minutes of arduous ascent the path crosses a road. A good 10 minutes later a track is reached on the right, which is followed onwards. After 20 minutes a plateau dominated by vineyards is reached where an unsurfaced road is crossed. 100 metres later another pista is crossed. Here the path joins up with the return route to the Volcán San Antonio car park coming to the left from Teneguía (straight on, see above).

The Caldera de Taburiente

Breathtaking panoramic mountains and a rugged crater basin

The Playa de Taburiente with its wonderful mountain frame.

The Caldera de Taburiente is one of the greatest, most spectacular erosion craters in the world and and to a certain extent forms the heart of the island. It was declared a National Park in 1954 and is dominated by wild streams, waterfalls and an evergreen landscape cut into by barrancos. Moreover the Caldera, which is fully isolated from other parts of the island, protects what is the most significant Guanch sacred area on the island – the Roque Idafe. The crater basin, which is 10km in diameter with rock walls of up to 1500m in height, is only reached with difficulty – in the Barranco de las Angustias the streams, which inside the Caldera join to form the Río Taburiente, have managed to break their way through to the sea. This deeply cut gorge provides the visitor with the best and shortest access to the Playa de Taburiente, the centre of the Caldera, but only on paths, as the rough unsurfaced road from Los Llanos ends before the actual basin at the viewpoint of Los Brecitos. A further point of access to the Caldera is available from the splendid look out point of the Cumbrecita, a route that is strictly reserved for walkers who are experienced in mountains, are sure-footed and have a head for heights.

The Caldera is surrounded by an over 2000m high horseshoe shaped ridge of mountains – the most significant section is the Cumbre de los Andenes, which has the highest point of the island, the Roque de los Muchachos, 2426m in height. On the northeast side this splendid area of high mountains is opened up via the Caldera High Road, which leads from Hoya Grande up to Roque de los Muchachos. From the road or the nearby viewpoints such as the Mirador de los Andenes there are fantastic views down into the Caldera and towards the east coast. Unfortunately this has destroyed a number of ascent routes from the coastal region, which have only partly been restored. Nevertheless there are numerous splendid walking opportunities all around the Caldera mountain chain, whether to the summit with the best views, the Pico Bejenado, to the Refugio de la Punta de los Roques or to the highest summits on La Palma; not to forget the adventurous grand circuit of the Caldera, which in two days of walking leads the ambitious walker over nearly all the summits of the Caldera area.

STARTING POINTS FOR WALKS

Los Brecitos, 1030m

Best starting point for walks in the Caldera (shortest access), but nevertheless only reached over a very bumpy unsurfaced road. No bus connection and no taxi driver will drive along the track; therefore inhabitants who are keen to do business offer a transfer in the morning from the car park at Barranco de las Angustias to Los Brecitos (2000: 1500 pesetas). The approach from Los Llanos (via Calle Dr. Fleming) to the car park shortly before the streambed of the Barranco de las Angustias is sign-posted »Caldera« (5km, partly gravel road). This is the starting point for walkers who want to go through the Barranco de las Angustias in the direction of Playa de Taburiente. To go to Los Brecitos, cross the streambed (after heavy rain sometimes impassable) and drive on up the other side to the end of the unsurfaced road (16km / about 4 hours on foot from the bus station in Los Llanos; small parking area, splendid view of the Caldera).

La Cumbrecita, 1287m

Car park with information booth at the end of the tarmac road which goes off from the main Santa Cruz – Los Llanos road, about 3.5km above El Paso at the Centro de Visitantes de El Paso (8km, no bus connection, 2 hrs on foot from the Centro de Visitantes de El Paso, stop for number 1 bus). Fantastic Caldera view from the nearby viewpoint of Mirador de las Chozas and Mirador Punta de los Roques.

Caldera High Road

From Santa Cruz de La Palma (via Mirca) as from Hoya Grande at Santo Domingo de Garafía, a tarmac road, narrow and extremely winding, leads up to the observatories as well as the highest point of the island, the Roque de los Muchachos, 2426m (car park with information booth, no bus connection, 42km from Santa Cruz, 14km from turn off on the Los Llanos – Santo Domingo de Garafía road at Hoya Grande.

37 From Los Brecitos to Playa de Taburiente

Easiest access to the Caldera

Los Brecitos – Playa de Taburiente – Cascada de la Fondada and back (or descent through the Barranco de las Angustias)

Location: Los Llanos de Aridane, 344m (bus stop for buses 1-5).

Starting point: Los Brecitos, 1030m, 16km from Los Llanos (Mirador, car park) – jeep transport also available to Los Brecitos from the Barranco de las Angustias car park (after 5km), in the morning.

Walking time: Los Brecitos – Playa de Taburiente 1½ hrs, Playa – Fondada Waterfall and back 1½ hrs, Playa – Los Brecitos 1¾ hrs; total time 4¾ hrs (with descent to the Barranco de las Angustias car park: 6¼ hrs).

Ascent: To Playa de Taburiente 300m, from the Playa de Taburiente to Fondada Waterfall good 300m, to Barranco de las Angustias car park 550m.

Grade: Easy walking on a good path as far as Playa de Taburiente, but the ascent to the Fondada Waterfall and the descent through the Barranco de las Angustias require absolute sure-footedness (steep, narrow sections).

Camping: A tent can be put up on the campsite at the Playa de Taburiente (previous permission from the National park needed).

Alternatives: From Mirador Cascada de la Fondada to Hoyo Verde (narrow, steep path; 1 hr one-way, 350m of ascent): From the Mirador a steep path begins. After a few minutes there is a short section where the path follows the narrow edge of the ridge, which drops steeply into the gorge and where care is required. At a path crossing after just a quarter of an hour go straight on uphill (to the right another fine view into the depths of the gorge). Shortly afterwards the path bends right towards the hill and then after 5 min splits on the edge towards the barranco. Here go uphill to the left, crossing a barranco runnel after

a few minutes. Shortly afterwards another barranco runnel is reached, which the path goes up for a short distance, then leaving it on the left for the nearby Pinar de Siete Fuentes (sign, splendid view). 25m above the sign the path forks: go straight on over the mountain ridge. Somewhat below the rock walls the path bears to the right towards the hillside. It now gradually leaves the pine forest and goes, at first somewhat exposed, right along the base of the cliffs with a splendid view over the Caldera. After 20 min it goes around an arête and drops down into a ruggedly romantic small valley (1360m) with several waterfalls, flanked by rock walls towering up to the sky.

From the Playa de Taburiente to the Cantos or into the Verduras Gorge (often without a path over boulders in the stream bed): ¼ hr above the campsite at the upper end of the Playa de Taburiente the valley splits. To the left the more rugged Barranco de los Cantos goes up, to the right the Barranco Verduras de Alfonso. Barranco de los Cantos: Upstream (at first the stream is subterranean) after ½ hr the Barranco Hoyo de Verde joins from the left (ascent possible almost to the foot of the Fondada Waterfall, 15 min). Further into the Barranco de los Cantos numerous small cascades and deep rock pools are passed and after ½ hr the terrain becomes more and more overgrown and rough. The ascent into the Barranco Verduras de Alfonso is somewhat more monotonous and after 1 hr the terrain also becomes overgrown and pathless, so that one is forced to go onto the path on the right above the streambed – just up here at this point the most beautiful cascades and deep rock pools are found.

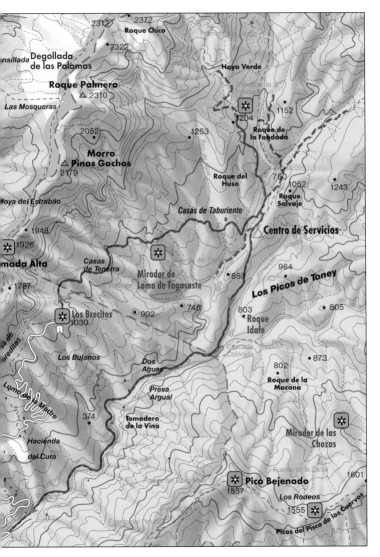

Degollada de las Palomas

nsillada

Roque Chico
2372
2312
2322

Hoyo Verde

Roque Palmero
△ 2310

Las Mosqueras

Cascada de la
Fondada

1152

※

1204

2052

1253

Roque de
la Fondada

Morro
△ Pinos Gachos
2179

Roque del
Huso

750

1052

1243

Hoya del Estrabito

Roque
Salvaje

Casas de Taburiente

1948

※ 1926

Centro de Servicios

Casas
de Tenerra

※

mada Alta

1787

Mirador de
Lomo de Tagasaste

853

964

Los Picos de Toney

805

745

803

902

Roque
Idafe

※ Los Brecitos
1030

R

Los Bujanos

Dos
Aguas

Cascada
Colorada

873

802

Roque de la
Mocana

s de
areditas

Presa
Argual

Tomadero
de la Vina

Mirador de las
Chozas

374

Loma de la Madre

Hacienda
del Cura

Fuente de la Zarza

1601

※ Pico Bejenado
1857

Los Rodeos

1555 ※

Picos del Pisco de los Cuervos

137

Mighty rock shapes accompany the walker on this excursion – above the rock towers of Los Agujeritos, to the right the Roque del Huso.

The splendid, exceptionally well-made descent path from Los Brecitos provides the shortest and easiest access to the Caldera. From the Playa de Taburiente, on which a campsite and a service centre for the National Park are found, there are various possibilities for excursions. Particularly beautiful is the detour to the Cascada de la Fondada, the highest waterfall on the island. Ambitious walkers who have arrived at Los Brecitos on the jeep from the car park in the Barranco de las Angustias can return to the car park via the »Gorge of the fear of death« – one of the most splendid excursions on La Palma.

Already from **Los Brecitos** a splendid view into the Caldera can be enjoyed. The wide path in the direction of the Caldera, at first protected by railings, is well signposted (»Zona de Acampada«). It leads gently downhill, soon crossing various wooden bridges in the Barranco del Ciempies and is mainly in the shade of mighty pine trees, with a wonderfully soft carpet of needles. Now in the National Park area the path crosses the Barranco de las Cañeras and reaches the small fern-covered plateau of Lomo de Tenerra. From here it is nearly all downhill. Go past the ruggedly-beautiful stream beds of the Barranco de la Traves and the Barranco de las Piedras Redondas, which very rarely carry any water, and after three-quarters of an hour the **Mirador de Lomo del Tagasaste**, a point with splendid views of the Caldera and the Roque Idafe, is reached. Shortly after, the Fuente de la Mula is passed via a wooden bridge, followed by the Barranco del Risco Liso and the Barranco de Bombas de Agua. The path leads now in a wide leftwards curve below the Casas de Taburiente and drops down to the **Playa de Taburiente**, 750m.

Shortly before the wide stream bed a fork in the path is reached with walking signs: to the right the path goes via the Taburiente streams to the campsite (Zona de Acampada) with the Centro de Servicios de Taburiente, to the left to the Cascada de la Fondada. The left-hand path forks again shortly after and the left-hand path again is

taken (Sign: »Hoyo Verde«). Steeply in narrow zigzags the path leads upwards to the foot of the Roque del Huso. After a good 20 minutes there is a beautiful viewpoint with a view of the Roque del Huso, on the summit of which two pine trees cling: not so imposing on this side, but so close that you can almost reach it. In parts protected by railings and with a fantastic view down onto the Playa de Taburiente, the path continues along the somewhat airy edge of the crest of the ridge, then goes straight on along a streambed, which is crossed twice. The path then stays to the right, through a green hollow to the nearby **Mirador Cascada de la Fondada,** 1050m, which is protected by railings. Directly opposite the dead straight, almost 100m high waterfall plunges into a deep rocky gorge. Fit walkers can continue on further upwards to the Hoyo Verde, a wonderful valley basin (→Alternatives). The main walk now goes back to **Playa de Taburiente**, where it is possible to allow oneself a refreshing swim in one of the paddling pools (the most beautiful rock pools are upstream, →Walk 38).

Descent through the Barranco de las Angustias (3¼ hrs): The signposted walk begins directly above the campsite to the left of the Centro de Servicios de Taburiente. It leads gently up and down across the hillside above the Taburiente stream and after about 5 minutes leads leftwards along a col to the neighbouring Barranco Almendro Amargo. After a few minutes it goes up a few metres to the **Somada de El Paso** (sign), then finally dips down across the slope above the gorge with fine views to the Roque Idafe. After a good half an hour the path goes rightwards close to the

stream. It now goes up somewhat and splits. The walker without a head for heights will continue rightwards along the normal signposted path (otherwise one can continue left »atajo«). Both paths join up after just 5 minutes at the section called **Las Lajitas del Viento** (sign). A few minutes later the Barranco Rivanceras (Amarillo) joins up from the left; here it is worthwhile making a detour to the left to the Cascada de Colores (→Walk 38). The walk now gradually leads down to the stream, which from here on is followed down the valley. After a few minutes, shortly after leaving the National Park area, the Río Almendro Amargo joins up with the Río Taburiente, which comes from the right (**Dos Aguas**, 425m; 1¼ hrs in total) – here begins the Barranco de las Angustias.

Cross over the Taburiente stream (depending on the water level it may be necessary to remove one's shoes and wade across) and follow the path which runs along the right-hand side of the valley, somewhat above the streambed. After a few minutes it returns to the streambed and goes down along this, continually changing from one side to the other. Along the way bathing pools invite one to take a rest. After a quarter of an hour the path goes under a water pipe bridge. About 40m later a path goes off left, but the cliff sections on it can be avoided via the narrow stream-

The Cascada de la Fondada, the highest waterfall on the island.

The Hoyo Verde, one of the most beautiful places in the Caldera.

bed (when the water is low, this and the following turnings off can be avoided, somewhat laboriously, by walking along the streambed). The path soon goes back to the streambed to leave it again to the left after a good 50m. 5 minutes later it returns to the streambed. A few minutes later the path goes back over to the left side of the valley, but after 5 minutes it crosses over the stream and continues on the right side of the valley. After just 10 minutes, above a canal bridge an open stone house (simple refuge) is reached at Morro de la Era. Shortly after the path crosses a canal and then returns to the streambed, which then leads immediately under another canal bridge. A good 5 minutes later, just after the narrow section, a path goes off again to the left (the continuation path through the streambed cannot be recommended, particularly when the water is high, as further down a rock step has to be overcome). It crosses the stream after a good 10 minutes (30m to the right is a beautiful rock arch and a cascade) and leads now for a further 10 minutes on the right side of the valley. After this the walk continues in the gravel bed of the gradually widening gorge down to the unsurfaced road from Los Llanos to Los Brecitos (just ½ hr) which leads over to the nearby **car park** of Barranco de las Angustias, 250m.

38 Through the Angustias Gorge to the Playa de Taburiente

A must for every walker!

Barranco de las Angustias – Dos Aguas (– Cascada de Colores) – Playa de Taburiente and back

Location: Los Llanos de Aridane, 344m (bus stop for buses 1-5).

Starting point: Car park at the streambed of the Barranco de las Angustias, 250m (5km from Los Llanos, partly unsurfaced road; good 1 hr on foot).

Walking time: Car park – Dos Aguas 2¼ hrs, Dos Aguas – Playa de Taburiente 1½ hrs, Playa de Taburiente – Dos Aguas 1¼ hrs, Dos Aguas – Car park 2 hrs; total time 7 hrs (detour to Cascada de Colores an additional ½ hr).

Ascent: About 550m.

Grade: Generally easy but long and tiring full-day walk – early start strongly recommended. In some sections sure-footedness and a head for heights needed.

Camping: Tents can be put up on the official area (Lugar de Acampada) at the Playa de Taburiente (permission required from the Centro de Visitantes de El Paso).

Alternatives: Jeep transfer from the Barranco de las Angustias car park to Los Brecitos offers the possibility to combine the walk with →Walk 37 (descent from Los Brecitos to Playa de Taburiente) one of the most magnificent undertakings on the island. Fom Playa de Taburiente there are numerous connecting walks (→Walk 37).

Advice: It is rare for the Angustias stream to have any water in it as far as the starting point at the car park. Should this, however, be the case then it is best to avoid this walk.

The walk through the Barranco de las Angustias in the Caldera de Taburiente is an adventure in itself. Almost half of the walk runs through the deeply cut gorge, frequently with sky-high cliffs flanking the sides, and in which there is one rock pool after another – some of these bathing pools are actually big enough to allow one to swim a few strokes. The ascent out of the barranco which follows, allows an impressive insight into the rugged world of gorges, rock needles and pine woods in the centre of the Caldera – a completely-isolated nature paradise, which would be almost oppressive were it not for the cheerful, branching Taburiente stream in the middle of the erosion crater. Paddling pools in the stream and the meadow at the campsite invite one to take a rest.

From the car park go directly up the gravel bed of the **Barranco de las Angustias**. Soon the first narrowing is reached: rock walls hem the stream into a bed only a few metres wide, and there are boulders too. After just half an hour a path goes off left before such a narrowing; when the water is low one can however, confidently continue walking and hopping. Only at the next narrowing, a few minutes later, is one forced to take the path branching off right (sign) – a rock step after about 30m, which is difficult to overcome, and over which a cascade pours when there is plenty of water, forces this detour (a beautiful rock arch before the rock step). Whoever prefers easier tracks and paths to the sometimes rather arduous walking along the bed of the barranco (now and then easy scrambling) does best to follow the path which crosses the streambed at a number of points (watch out for signs), and which avoids the narrow sections. Staying in the streambed, however, a dam wall is reached after a good hour. Here scramble up to the left and af-

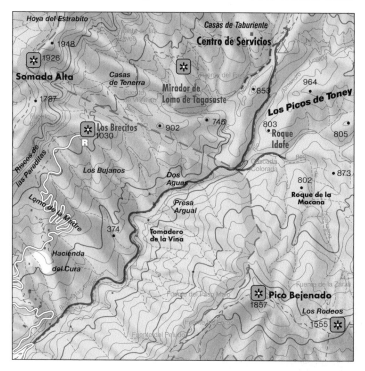

terwards balance over the canal bridge to the right side of the stream (if this is too airy, the path goes immediately left above this). After a total of 2 hours a further dam wall is reached (the water from the blocked off streams is diverted through a ring canal) which is avoided to the left. Shortly after the junction of the Río Taburiente from the left and the Río Almendro Amargo is reached: **Dos Aguas**, 425m.

It is necessary to go straight on so the Taburiente stream has to be crossed (depending on the water level it may be necessary to take off one's shoes and wade through). Just 5 minutes after the stream-crossing the ascent path to the Playa de Taburiente goes off left (Sign: »Al Lugar de Acampada«) – In order to make a detour to **Cascada de Colores** just continue along the streambed. Right at the beginning a cascade of Río Almendro Amargo can be seen on the left. The artificial dam step with the »coloured cascade« is reached after 15 minutes along the bed, which contains iron and is ochre-coloured (some easy scrambling). The waterfall could be climbed on the right, but the continuation in this especially protected area of the park is not permitted.

Return to the ascent to the Playa de Taburiente: The path, which is easy at first, soon reaches the section called **Las Lajitas del Viento** in which it splits

Rest at the Playa de Taburiente.

into two for a short while, an easier (Camino normal) and a more difficult variant (atajo: only for those who do not suffer from vertigo). It now winds its way up more steeply. The rock needle of Roque Idafe draws ever nearer and down below there is the rushing sound of the Río Almendro Amargo – and gradually the view of the mighty Caldera opens out. 1¼ hours after Dos Aguas the sweaty ascent through the open pine forest comes to an end, after passing the section called **Cuesta del Reventón** and

A worthwhile detour leads along the foot of the Roque Idafe to the Cascada de Colores – the water in the stream contains a lot of iron.

the splendid viewpoint of **Somada de El Paso**. From the col it is only 15 minutes to the Playa, the vegetation suddenly becomes more lush: ferns, deciduous trees and pines are found. From the shady meadow sites on the official camping area with the Centro de Servicios de Taburiente a path leads down to the wide streambed of the **Playa de Taburiente**, 750m. The most beautiful cascades and bathing pools are by the way in the Taburiente stream below the Playa. They are reached via a path at the lower end of the campsite (railing) which leads down the valley to the left to the stream – the first rock pools are reached after about 10 minutes. The hardly visible path, in places marked with cairns, continues for about a quarter of an hour down the valley to the Cueva de las Palomas/Hoyo de los Juncos (cascade).

39 From the Cumbrecita to Escuchadero

Eindrucksvolle Höhenwanderung an den Calderahängen

Cumbrecita – Mirador Punta de los Roques – Galería Aridane – Galería la Faya – Hoyo de los Pinos – Lomo del Escuchadero and back

Location: El Paso, 664m (bus stop for bus 1).

Starting point: Car park on the Cumbrecita, 1287m.

Walking time: Cumbrecita – Galería Aridane good ½ hr, Galería Aridane – Galería la Faya 40 min, Galería la Faya – Hoyo de los Pinos 20 min, Hoyo de los Pinos – Escuchadero 50 min, return route 2¼ hrs; total time 4¾ hrs.

Ascent: 350m.

Grade: Sure-footedness and a head for heights are absolute requirements for the path, which in places is narrow, sloping and occasionally even rather exposed. Important advice: Do not leave the path under any circumstances. Numerous sections are affected by possible landslip or stonefall, so before beginning the walk one should go to the National Park Information booth to check on the current state of the paths – after heavy rain the walk should be completely avoided.

Alternative: Continuation from Escuchadero to Playa de Taburiente: This path is only for the experienced walker and demands absolute sure-footedness and a good head for heights. The sections which cross steep slopes become even more worrying and unpredictable than before and the direction of the path is less clear. However, the walker who nevertheless wishes to undertake this difficult walk in the Caldera de Taburiente should at least check on the condition of the paths

before commencing (according to the state of the paths one should allow at least 3 hrs walking time to the Playa de Taburiente, plus another good 3 hrs for the return walk, assuming that one does not intend to spend the night in the Caldera).

Combination possible with Walk 40.

From the Cumbrecita a wide path leads leftwards past the information booth of the National Park administration down to an information board. From here a path leads down to the left which forks after a few minutes. Stay right here and follow the signs »Zona de Acampada« (left, and shortly after to the right leads to the nearby Mirador Punta de los Roques). Shortly after the path goes around the edge of a drop – now with a splendid view to the Cal-

The narrow path leads along the steeply sloping rock and scree flank of the Caldera.

dera – from Bejenado over the Roque Idafe and the Fondada Waterfall as far as the Roque de los Muchachos. After a short descent below an unusual slabby wall the path splits once again. Keep right again. The path now leads across the hillside accompanied by a covered water channel and crosses a series of barrancos, which only seldom contain any water. In the meantime the path sticks closely to the cliffs and soon the **Galería Aridane** is reached. A few minutes later a stone hut belonging to canal workers is passed. The next point to aim for is the **Galería la Faya** (stone hut, gallery): the last section to reach this is again very narrow and exposed.

The continuation to the **Hoyo de los Pinos** should only be undertaken by absolutely sure-footed walkers who do not suffer from vertigo: there is a very unpleasant traverse across a steep scree slope, where the path is moreover, extremely narrow and sloping (chain protection). But the effort is worthwhile: a small waterfall awaits one – at least in the months with more rain – situated in the hollowed out small valley above the cascade.

The path now climbs up very steeply through the gorge (watch carefully for cairns and signs) and after a quarter of an hour turns towards the hillside. Apart from a couple short traverses, the path, which is now frequently very narrow and sloping, continues to go steeply uphill, at the end even requiring a little scrambling. Then the **Lomo de Escuchadero** (sign) is reached – a mighty, rocky mountain ridge, which reaches well down into the Caldera. Immediately after the sign, a path branches off left, leading over the crest in 5 minutes to a small rise on the ridge – a fantastic viewpoint with a stunning, panoramic view of the Caldera.

40 From the Cumbrecita to the Mirador de las Chozas

Easy circuit to perhaps the most well known view point on La Palma

Cumbrecita – Mirador de las Chozas – Mirador Punta de los Roques – Cumbrecita

Location: El Paso, 664m (bus stop for bus 1).
Starting point: Car park at the Cumbrecita, 1287m.
Walking time: 1 hr for the circuit.
Ascent: Only minimal amount of ascent/descent.
Grade: Easy walking on sufficiently wide paths and forestry roads – in wet conditions, the return path can, however, be unpleasant.
Combination possible with Walk 39.

In spring time clover transforms the forest floor into a yellow carpet of blossom.

Caldera view from the path near the Cumbrecita.

It would be an exaggeration to call this short excursion a proper walk. However, this leisurely stroll can be recommended to all keen walkers who would like to obtain an overview and a general impression of the mighty dimensions of the Caldera – and for this there is hardly a better, or more-easily accessible viewpoint than the Mirador de las Chozas.

From the car park at the **Cumbrecita** go back for a short distance along the tarmac road to the first left-hand bend, where on the right after crossing the paved car park, a wide unsurfaced road turns off. This almost level road leads in about 20 minutes to the two viewpoints at the **Mirador de las Chozas** protected by railings and situated at the far end of the turning area. Afterwards go back the few metres to where the road splits. Here a path goes off left, which crosses the hillside by mainly easy walking and two footbridges and leads down into a weakly defined hollow. After a few metres of ascent, a path junction is reached. Stay left here to the **Mirador Punta de los Roques** – the viewing point is hardly inferior to that of the Mirador de las Chozas. From here go back to the path junction, uphill here (sign »La Cumbrecita«) and go right at the next junction up to the **Cumbrecita**.

41 Pico Bejenado, 1857m

Mountain walk onto La Palma's only »real« summit

(Centro de Visitantes –) El Barrial – El Rodeo – Pico Bejenado and back

Location: El Paso, 664m (bus stop for bus 1).

Starting point: Car park almost at the end of the tarmac road from the National Park Visitor Centre – Valencia – El Barrial, 1150m: From the El Paso – Santa Cruz main road at the Centro de Visitantes (bus-stop) go left in the Cumbrecita direction, going straight on after 1km, and shortly after at the right hand turn for Cumbrecita continue leftwards in the direction of Valencia (sign »Sendero del Bejenado 7km«). After a few kilometres the tarmac road becomes a bumpy unsurfaced road; the car park is found shortly after the road becomes tarmac again (Sign: »Bejenado«); 8km from the Visitor Centre (2hrs on foot).

Walking time: Ascent 2¼ hrs, descent 1¾ hrs; total time 4 hrs (from Centro de Visitantes an extra 3½ hrs).

Ascent: Good 700m.

Grade: Easy mountain walking on well maintained little path – here and there slightly slippery sections.

Refreshment: Restaurant Las Piedras at the Centro de Visitantes.

Alternatives: Descent possibility on return route via the ridge top on the edge of the Caldera: The clearly visible, narrow path goes off left about 7 min after El Rodeo. It climbs up for a short distance to the top of the crest and then continues rightwards on the other side of the crest of Roque de los Cuervos undulating across the hillside. After a good ½ hr there is a possible detour to a viewpoint (iron stake) with a view of the Cumbrecita. Now go down along the high section curving down to the right (cairns) very steep and slippery in parts. After a few minutes the path becomes an increasingly wide cart track, which is followed continually downhill to

the Pista Ferrer, which is reached after passing the National Park sign. This leads back to the car park in a few minutes (1½ hrs from El Rodeo).

Detour to the rock engravings of Tamarahoya: From the Bejenado path turn off (see below) continue for about 10 min along the Pista Ferrer as far as a sharp right-hand bend with many boulders on the left side. A number of boulders with spiral prehistoric rock engravings can be found on, and two metres below, the path which leads on down the mountain ridge.

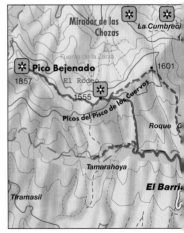

Caldera view from the summit of Pico Bejenado.

The Bejenado is perhaps the most beautiful and moreover one of the most popular panoramic summits on the island. It can be described as the only prominent summit on La Palma and not only provides a unique view of the Caldera and its surroundings but also of the Cumbres in the south and a large part of the west coast.

Follow the forestry track, which leads uphill from the **car park** (walks notice board). After 10 minutes a **National Park sign** is passed. Here continue completely to the left along the gently rising forestry road (Pista Ferrer). After a further 20 minutes a cart track goes off to the right to Bejenado (sign; straight on it is possible to take a detour to the Tamarahoya prehistoric rock engravings) soon becoming a beautiful well looked after path. After about 10 minutes the path splits (a signpost indicates a fenced off rock engraving site about 130 metres off to the right). The walk continues uphill along the left fork. After a total of about 1¼ hrs the crest of the ridge and thereby the Caldera edge is reached: the viewpoint is called **El Rodeo**. The view down into the Caldera is simply fantastic. Now the path leads to the south flank and leads in wide hairpins easily up to the summit of **Pico Bejenado** (1 hr from El Rodeo). The best viewing point is perhaps a short distance behind the summit by the trigonometry pillar: from here the view opens out onto the Barranco de las Angustias as well as to the Caldera.

42 From Reventón to the Refugio de la Punta de los Roques, 2040m

A super quality walk

Reventón Pass – Pico Ovejas – Pico Corralejo – Refugio de la Punta de los Roques and back

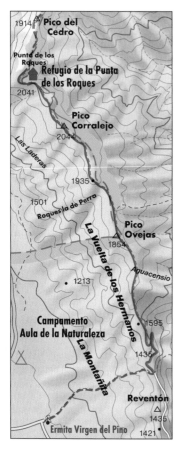

Location: El Paso, 664m, or Breña Alta, 344m (bus number 1 stops at both).

Starting point: Reventón Pass, 1410m, to the north of Reventón, 1435m. Reached by a bumpy 6.5km long unsurfaced road, the turn off to which is near Refugio El Pilar.

Walking time: Reventón Pass – Pico Ovejas 1¼ hrs, Pico Ovejas – Pico Corralejo ¾ hr, Pico Corralejo – Refugio de la Punta de los Roques ½ hr, descent 1¾ hrs; total time 4¼ hrs.

Ascent: Good 600m.

Grade: Generally easy and straight forward walking, only a bit steep at the end.

Alternative: Ascent and descent from the Ermita Virgen del Pino to the Reventón Pass an extra 1¾ hrs (→Walks 29, 30).

One thing should be said straight away: this splendid walk should really begin at the Ermita de la Virgen del Pino. But as is always the case, once there is a road every metre and every hour is cheated on. From consideration for the majority of walkers the more popular shorter ascent from the Reventón Pass is therefore described. Instead of a sweaty ascent to the crest of the Cumbre a mere half hour of being shaken about has to be taken into consideration…

Past the antenna decorated Reventón the car is parked at the split in the unsurfaced road (at the

View from Corralejo of the Punta de los Roques – the refuge hut is to the left.

end of the almost level top of the crest) – the **Reventón Pass**, 1410m.
Follow the rising track to the left (Sign »Pico de la Nieve«), which after a quarter of an hour becomes a mainly wide path, marked here and there with a red stripe. It mainly follows the line of the crest, thereby offering splendid views to all sides. The trees en route are Xmas trees even decorated with hanging moss, while rock roses and tree heaths dominate the scrub. The **Pico Ovejas**, 1854m, more an orientation point than a peak, is the first hurdle on the walk. Almost immediately it goes up to the next rise. After some time the **Pico Corralejo**, 2044m, is also reached. Here it is worthwhile making a detour (only a few minutes) to the right up to the highest point, from which almost the whole of the Caldera ridge can be viewed. In front the Punta de los Roques with the refuge hut of the same name can already be seen. The path now leads to the left of the ridge top and down a little (short steep section) with a splendid view of the Cumbrecita and then goes up more steeply to the **Refugio de la Punta de los Roques**. The small stone hut, newly built in the year 2000, is eagerly visited by Palmeros at the weekends – it is ideal for a substantial picnic. It is certainly worthwhile to make the short ascent to the nearby **Punta de los Roques**, 2085m, which gives a unique view of the Caldera and its surroundings. However, only experienced mountaineers should venture onto this pathless summit.

43 Pico de la Nieve, 2239m

A visit to the classic panoramic summit of the island and a detour to the meeting place of the island's original inhabitants are a must

Pista Pico de la Nieve – Pico de la Nieve – Pico de la Veta de la Arena – Pista Pico de la Nieve

Starting point: Sign-posted left-hand turn off »Pista Pico de la Nieve« from the Santa Cruz – Roque de los Muchachos road (at Km 22.5), 1870m, or car park at the end of the pothole filled unsurfaced road (then a good ¾ hr shorter). No bus connection.

Walking time: Pista – car park – Pico de la Nieve 1¼ hrs, Pico de la Nieve – Pico de la Sabina just ½ hr, Pico de la Sabina – car park – Pista just 1 hr; total time 2½ hrs.

Ascent: 360m (or 220m from car park at the end of the pista).

Grade: Easy mountain walking, although some mountain slopes are crossed where sure-footedness and a head for heights are necessary.

Combination possible with Walks 44 and 45.

The Pico de la Nieve (»Snow peak«) is undoubtedly the most visited elevation on the complete crater circuit – if the Roque de los Muchachos is disregarded. And not without reason: the summit plateau that drops away steeply to the Caldera offers a splendid view of the giant erosion crater and of the east coast. Snow however, as promised by the name will be sought here in vain – even in the »deepest« winter there are few days where it can compete with the sun of the Canaries.

It is best to abstain from driving the last section along the bumpy pista and to park straight away at the turning off from the tarmac road. Then either follow the obvious path 10m to the right of the turning off (somewhat shorter) or follow the pista itself (just 2km) up to the **car park** at the end of the unsurfaced road. The sign indicates the way forward, which for the first few metres is accompanied by a railing. It first cuts across the hillside in a southerly direction and then ascends in a leisurely fashion. Just a quarter of an hour from the car park a fork is reached. Here follow the rising right-hand path to the Pico de la Nieve (sign). The pines now thin out and instead there are the laburnums, which are typical for this altitude. At the height of the crest (beautiful lookout point) the ascent path joins the white-red marked Caldera High Route, which is then followed to the right. After just a few minutes a sign-posted path goes off left to the summit plateau.

In the foreground encompassed by the boulders is the assembly place, »La Erita«, and in the background on the right is the Pico de la Nieve.

From **Pico de la Nieve** go to the white-red marked high route and follow this to the right. Ignore the turn off from the ascent route and instead continue along the crest (Direction: Refugio de la Punta de los Roques / Ermita de la Virgen del Pino). Soon there is another turning off (sign, to the left one could return to the starting point) –here too follow the white-red marked ridge walk, which 10 minutes later, shortly before the summit of the **Pico de la Veta de la Arena**, switches over to the side of the ridge facing the Caldera, just after the Degollado del Barranco de la Madera has been passed. Instead of taking the path which leads to the other side of the ridge, go straight along the top of the ridge to **La Erita**, which is already visible, a meeting place for the Guanches which is surrounded by a metal fence. The assembly place is surrounded by rock walls on two sides and has a diameter of about 20m. On both rock walls, but particularly on the one behind, numerous rock engravings are preserved, despite the strong weathering on the wind and weather exposed ridge and despite vandalism. After this detour go back to the last split in the path (10 min; sign) and this time follow the right-hand path via a sometimes unpleasant, steep traverse of the hillside, which leads back to the car park at the end of the Nieve Pista. Go back down this to the starting point.

44 From Pico de la Nieve to Ermita Virgen del Pino

Long descent along one of the showpiece walks of the island

Pista Pico de la Nieve – Pico de la Sabina – Refugio de la Punta de los Roques – Reventón Pass – Ermita de la Virgen del Pino

Starting point: Signposted left-hand turn off »Pista Pico de la Nieve« from the Santa Cruz – Roque de los Muchachos road (at Km 22.5), 1870m or car park at the end of the pista (then ½ hr shorter). No bus connection, approach drive by taxi.

Destination: Ermita de la Virgen del Pino, 900m, or Centro de Visitantes, 870m (bus stop for bus 1), on the main road from El Paso to Santa Cruz.

Walking time: Pista – car park – La Erita 1¼ hrs, La Erita – Refugio de la Punta de los Roques 1½ hrs, Refugio de la Punta de los

Roques – Reventón Pass 1¾ hrs, Reventón Pass – Ermita Virgen del Pino ¾ hr, Ermita Virgen del Pino – Centro de Visitantes ½ hr; total time 5½ hrs.

Ascent: 1350m of descent, 350m of ascent.

Grade: Generally easy ridge walking, but nevertheless long, requiring fitness, somewhat steep only in parts, but a few exposed scree sections.

Refreshment: Only at the end of the walk in the Bar-restaurant Las Piedras, opposite the Visitor Centre.

Combination possible with Walk 43.

The descent from the Caldera Ridge to the Ermita de la Virgen del Pino leads through various vegetation zones: in the high areas the laburnum scrub is dominant on the otherwise bare ridge heights; a level lower are the open pine forests and then the laurel forests on the slopes of the Cumbre Nueva. The views from this walk are also uniquely beautiful: the Caldera, the east coast and also the Aridane Valley lie at the walker's feet.

The walk starts at the beginning of the Pista Pico de la Nieve. After just 2km the **car park** is reached at the end of the forestry road. The path keeps to the left and gently goes up across the mountain slope. Just a quarter of an hour after leaving the car park a fork in the path is reached. To the right it goes up to Pico de la Nieve (worthwhile detour) – stay, however on the straight path which leads over steep folds in the hill, which are unpleasantly sloping in parts, up to the top of the ridge. Shortly before the top of the ridge a white-red marked path is reached which is followed to the left (sign: »Ermita de la Virgen del Pino«). 10 minutes after the fork the main path swings over to the right side of the ridge. Here it is recommended to go straight on along

the old path. After a few minutes the fenced off Meeting place of the Guanches: **La Erita** is passed (prehistoric rock etchings) at the **Pico de la Veta de la Arena**, 2137m. Shortly after one is back on the marked path again which gradually goes down past the Pico de la Sabina into the breche of the **Degollada del Río** (sign; beautiful view down the barranco to Las Nieves). This is followed by a short but strenuous ascent over a steep scree slope and a slightly rising traverse, finally reaching the foot of the Punta de los Roques, 2085m and then the **Refugio de la Punta de los Roques**, 2040m.

From the refuge hut the path leads over to the neighbouring **Corralejo**, 2044m and onwards along the top of the ridge always to the south in the direction of the **Reventón Pass**, 1410m. This panoramic section of the walk through open pine forest is undoubtedly one of the finest walks that La Palma has to offer. Shortly before the pass the path becomes a forestry road joining a wide unsurfaced road at the height of the pass. Immediately the camino real goes off right to **Ermita Virgen del Pino** (sign), and leads down to the church through laurel and scrub forest. It is only just half an hour from here to the bus stop at the visitor centre on the main road (go on down the tarmac road, and left at the crossing).

45 Over the Pico de la Nieve to Pico de la Cruz, 2351m

Leisurely high walk over the Caldera with fine views

Pista Pico de la Nieve – Pico de la Nieve – Pico de la Cruz and back

Starting point: Signposted left-hand turn off »Pista Pico de la Nieve« from the Santa Cruz – Roque de los Muchachos road (at Km 22.5), 1870m, or car park at the end of the pista (then a good ¾ hr shorter). No bus connection.
Walking time: Pista – car park – Pico de la Nieve 1¼ hrs, Pico de la Nieve – Piedra

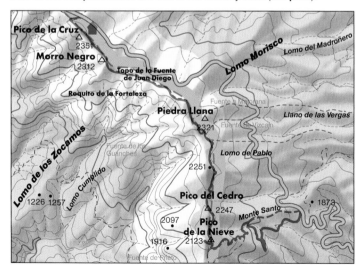

Llana 1 hr, Piedra Llana – Pico de la Cruz ¾ hr, return route 2½ hrs (return via the road 1 hr shorter); total time 5½ hrs.
Ascent: About 500m in total.
Grade: Easy-going high walk.
Combination possible with Walks 43, 44, 46, 47 and 48.

It is best to park at the beginning of the sign-posted »Pista Pico de la Nieve«, from where it is just 2km to the end of the forestry road (**car park**).

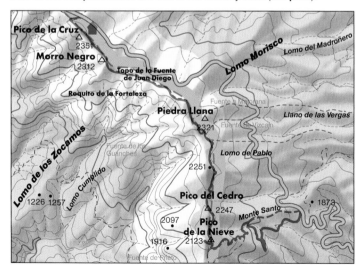

On the summit of Pico de la Nieve – in the distance is Teide.

The actual path, which splits after a quarter of an hour, begins here (sign). Follow the right hand path which ascends to Pico de la Nieve (sign). Once at the level of the crest, the ascent path joins the white-red marked Caldera circuit. Follow this to the right. After only a few minutes a sign-posted path to the **Pico de la Nieve**, 2239m, goes off to the left. Back again on the Caldera circuit, continue in a northerly direction. The beautiful, continually gentle Caldera circuit avoids the next elevation, the **Pico del Cedro**, 2247m, to the right, dips gently around and then goes up again a little. Down below to the right the nearby road to the Muchachos summit can be seen. After another weakly defined dip, the path goes up to the summit of the **Piedra Llana**, 2321m (short summit detour). Again and again there are splendid views of the Caldera, also on the continuation of the path to the Pico de la Cruz, whose tiny summit hut can be seen from a great distance. Below to the right, between the path and the road, a curious-looking metal cross can be seen. After a short section, it is only a few metres up through rocks to reach the summit of **Pico de la Cruz**, 2351m. This has some of the finest views of any of the Caldera summits, rising up as it does exactly opposite the deep notch of the Barranco de las Angustias, and thereby allowing a view right through the Angustias gorge as far as Puerto de Tazacorte.

The best way back is to follow the line of the ascent. However, it is possible to descend immediately after the summit to the tarmac road (a few minutes) and to go right along this back to the starting point (about 6km!).

46 From Pico de la Cruz to Los Sauces

Long descent through nearly all the vegetation zones on the island

High Road Km 29 – Mirador de las Barandas – Los Sauces (or Los Tilos / Barlovento)

Starting point: Km 29 on the High Road Santa Cruz – Muchachos, 2270m, at the foot of Pico de la Cruz (1km to the north of Mirador de Taburiente on the Degollada de Franceses). No bus connection.
Destination: Los Sauces, 266m (bus stop for buses 16 and 18).
Walking time: High Road – forestry road 1¾ hrs, Continuation to Mirador de las Barandas 1½ hrs, Mirador de las Barandas – Los Sauces 1¼ hrs; total time 4½ hrs (Pico de la Cruz an extra 20 min).
Ascent: 2000m of descent.
Grade: Very long, generally easy descent via paths and forestry roads, with only occasional steep sections.
Refreshment: Bar-Restaurants in Los Sauces.
Alternative: From the Mirador de las Barandas it is possible to descend to Barlovento (→Walk 14) or Los Tilos (→Walk 13).

Combination possible with Walks 45, 47, 48 and 50.
Advice: As there is no bus service to the High Road, it is best to make the approach by taxi.

This 2000 metre descent leads through heath landscapes as well as pine and laurel forests and offers wonderful views of the northeast with the Barranco del Agua. The starting point for the walk is the **High Road** at about Km 29, immediately at the foot of Pico de la Cruz, 2351m. To make an excursion to the summit of this fine panoramic mountain, it is necessary to go up the prominent camino as far as the Caldera circuit path, via which the summit hut is reached up to the left (10 min from the High Road). Back again at the High Road, follow this for about 50m in a northerly direction and then turn right onto the wide camino, which is bordered by stones. It is marked by occasional double white dots and by cairns and leads comfortably down over a mountain ridge. After just half an hour it leads into an open pine forest. The mountain ridge gradually narrows

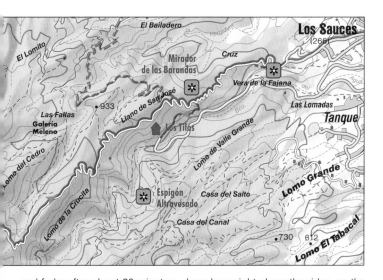

and forks after about 20 minutes – here bear right along the ridge on the edge of the precipitous Barranco del Agua. 20 minutes later the mountain ridge splits again – here continue along the ridge which bears off down to the left. The path now becomes somewhat overgrown and steeper. After a total of 1½ hrs of descent a forestry road is crossed, which is again crossed a few minutes later. The camino continues on down the mountain ridge, passes through a fine pine forest overgrown with ferns and finally after 15 minutes ends in a forestry road, which is followed downwards. Keep sharply right at the fork after 25m (two white dots), go across a minor valley and reach another fork after 45 minutes, bearing left here along the continuation of the forestry road. 10 minutes later, straight after a sharp left-hand bend, a paved path goes off to the right, which soon goes down through a small valley and meets up with the forestry road after a few minutes. In the continuation there are two further possible short cuts via the camino, or it is possible to stick with the forestry road (always keeping right). After a total of 1½ hrs on the forestry road a wide path goes off to the right to the 100m distant **Mirador de las Barandas**, 800m (sign) – however, stay on downwards along the forestry road, which after 45 minutes becomes a tarmac road. In **Los Sauces**, go directly down via the extremely steep road to a church (see Walk 13).

47 From Roque Faro to Pico de la Cruz, 2351m

Wonderful, but arduous ascent to the Cumbre High Road

Roque Faro – Lomo los Corraletes – Mirador de Taburiente (– Pico de la Cruz) and back

Starting point: Bar-Restaurant Los Reyes in Roque Faro, 1010m (bus stop for bus 11) on the main road from Santo Domingo de Garafía – Barlovento.

Walking time: Roque Faro – Col 2 hrs, Col – Mirador de Taburiente 1½ hrs, descent 3 hrs; total time 6½ hrs (Pico de la Cruz extra ¾ hr).

Ascent: 1250m (Pico de la Cruz extra 100m).

Grade: The steep ascent and descent requires a good level of fitness and sure-footedness – in winter when there is snow in the upper parts it is not recommended.

Refreshment: Bar-Restaurants in Roque Faro.

Combination possibility with Walks 16, 45, 46, 48 and 50.

Advice: In order to only do the descent, take a taxi to the Mirador de Taburiente (Degollada de Frances) on the High Road at Km 30 (no bus connection).

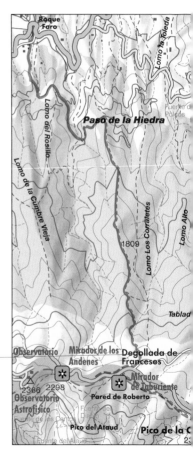

The area around Roque Faro is one of the most charming walking areas on La Palma: The landscape is dominated by extensive pine forests, lush meadows and laurel woods extending to the coast. High above, the mountains on the perimeter of the Caldera attract the walker, and thanks to the height of Roque Faro it is possible for fit mountain walkers to climb them in a day without a problem.

From the Bar-Restaurant Reyes in **Roque Faro** go up the village road for a good 5 minutes until a forestry road goes off left at the first large pine trees. It leads immediately up into the woods (short section paved) and then forks shortly afterwards. Go left here and straight on along the forestry road which leads gently up and down along the hillside (not downhill to the left, and not sharply uphill to the right). Finally it leads into a barranco and ends in half an hour immediately after a small house. Now take the camino which goes off to the left leading to the right past the house, and down into the barranco, crossing this via a bridge. It then goes up to a track on the other side (5 min). Follow this uphill to the right, leaving it after 2 minutes for a paved path that bears off left in a sharp right-hand bend. This leads quite steeply up the hillside, meets a track after 10 minutes, runs parallel to the right of the track and then begins to go uphill in hairpins. A few minutes later a sunny mountain ridge covered in ferns and rock roses is reached, the **Lomo los Corraletes**, which provides the continuation. Keep going up the steep, tree-free fire break up onto the top of the ridge (immediately crossing a forestry path at right angles to it). This is an extremely strenuous undertaking despite the zigzags on the steepest sections. It is only after 1¼ hrs that the ridge flattens out and now the path leads slightly downhill reaching a **col**, 1792m, just after a small rocky promontory. Here one should take a short rest and take in the mighty precipice of the Cumbre. Above this it goes on up, soon in hairpins. About 10 minutes above the col, the obvious path bordered by rocks splits – continue along the ascending camino (to the left a path goes through the cliff and the Barranco de Franceses, which begins here). Also keep to the left on the camino at the fork shortly after (do not go off right). It goes uphill steeply, only interrupted by a short leftwards traverse at the foot of a cliff, and it gradually leaves behind the last wind blown pines. Just an hour after the col, the path leads to the left of a beautiful lava wall; the High Road and the observatory get ever nearer now. 5 minutes later a small cave is passed, which has been converted into a camping and rest area. 20 minutes later the camino joins a forestry road coming up from Barlovento, which in 5 minutes leads to the High Road. Along this (right) it is only a few minutes to the **Mirador de Taburiente** (Degolada de Franceses), 2297m which permits a fantastic view into the Caldera and towards the north coast. To continue to the **Pico de la Cruz**, follow the camino, which goes up left over the crest of the Cumbre, opposite the junction with the High Road (just ½ hr one way).

48 Onto the Roque de los Muchachos, 2426m

Spectacular downward views from the path to the highest summit

Mirador de Taburiente – Pared de Roberto – Mirador de los Andenes – Observatories – Roque de los Muchachos and back

Starting point: The Mirador de Taburiente, which is protected by railings, 2297m (photographer road sign), at the Degollada de Franceses – about Km 30 on the High Road between Santa Cruz and Roque de los Muchachos. Fantastic Caldera view. No bus connection.

Walking time: Ascent 2 hrs, return 1¾ hrs; total time 3¾ hrs.

Ascent: About 250m.

Grade: Easy, relaxed walking – nevertheless, sure-footedness and a head for heights needed.

Alternative: Descent from Roque de los Muchachos to Tijarafe (one of the showpiece walks of the island but very arduous in view of the difficult line, great height difference and amount of ascent): The camino forks off from the road to Roque de los Muchachos at about 2200m, immediately above the helicopter landing site (sign: »El Pinar/Tijarafe 11km«, about 2km from the summit / 400m above the crossing on the High Road) and leads mainly downhill to the foot of the Caldera mountains (after about 1½ hrs a road goes off right to Tinizara) and later dips down noticeably to Tijarafe (about 4½ hrs from Roque de los Muchachos).

Combination possible with Walks 45, 46, 47 and 49.

Since the highest mountain on La Palma was opened up via a road, it has only had a limited attraction for walkers and mountaineers. Nevertheless, there are a number of paths which deserve interest, in particular the route described here along the edge of the crater, which continually spoils the walker with its views down into the Caldera de Taburiente.

To the right of the railings on the **Mirador de Taburiente** an obvious path with white-red markings (sign: »Roque de los Muchachos«) goes off on the side of the ridge facing the Caldera. It has views into the numerous gorges of the fissured Caldera with the Playa de Taburiente. Go past the arch in the **Pared de Roberto** (Robert Wall), the views downwards becoming more and more spectacular. There is an almost bird's eye view of the scree ribbon

Again and again en route there are fantastic views of the Caldera de Taburiente, the Pico Bejenado and the Cumbre Vieja.

on the Playa de Taburiente and the rock towers of Huso and Idafe stand out prominently. On the other side, the Pico Bejenado finishes off the wide round. Beyond it, almost an island to itself, is the Cumbre Vieja with its volcanic cores. After an hour the crest of the ridge is gained (to the right it is possible to make a detour to the **Mirador de los Andenes**: immediately to the right below is the road). The white-red Caldera circuit path now largely follows the line of the crest and the two **observatories** are left behind on the right. After only a few minutes the narrow viewpoint of the **Fuente Nueva**, 2366m, protected by railings, is reached. In the background it is possible to make out the neighbouring islands of Tenerife, La Goma and El Hierro. It is now only three-quarters of an hour from the highest point on the island. For a short while there is a road on the right, then the path goes through a last depression up to the ridge between the stone »boys« (Muchachos) and the silver domes of the observatories. In order to complete the last few metres to the summit of **Roque de los Muchachos**, 2426m, by avoiding the road, keep to the left. Right next to the summit car park and in front of the group of rocks at the highest point is an information booth belonging to the National Park administration. Before returning it is worth making a detour to the elevation, which drops down almost vertically towards the Caldera (10 minutes one way).

49 From the Roque de los Muchachos to Somada Alta, 1926m

Over barren scree slopes to a romantic unspoilt summit

Roque de los Muchachos – Roque Palmero – Morro Pinos Gachos – Somada Alta and back

Starting point: Car park at the summit of Roque de los Muchachos, 2426m (no bus connection).

Walking time: Roque de los Muchachos – Roque Palmero 1 hr, Roque Palmero – Somada Alta 1¼ hrs, return route 2¾ hrs; total time 5 hrs.

Ascent: About 600m.

Grade: Easy mountain walking.

Alternatives: Further descent via Hoya Grande and the Torre del Time to Mirador El Time, to La Punta or to El Jesús is possible (→Walks 50, 26).

Combination possible with Walk 48.

The Somada Alta is one of the most isolated elevations on the Caldera and it has some of the best views. It is a romantic place, the ridge decorated by pines and boulders, and it is possible to look directly down on the beginning of the Barranco de las Angustias. Only the approach is a bit dreary: it goes through desolate screes with hardly any vegetation.

From the Information booth at the **Roque de los Muchachos** take the white-red marked path, which goes down in a westerly direction over a scree slope to the road. Follow this to the left as far as the first sharp right-hand bend (10 min). Here a gravel track goes off to the left (sign »Torre del Time«), and immediately ends in front of a fenced off plot of land with a house and a steel construction. The path with its white-red markings continues on the right, going up and down across the scree slopes on the side of the ridge which faces away from the Caldera. Down below, a broad plateau overgrown with broom spreads out, thereby not permitting a view of the coast. It is only from the hollows in between elevations covered by lumps of rock that views into the depths of the Caldera can be glimpsed – but these views are incredible: it is repeatedly possible to see the rugged barrancos, deeply gouged out rock gorges and rubble bands which sometimes drop vertically from the Caldera. The first of these hollows (Degollada de Hoyo Verde) is reached shortly after the beginning of the path. Soon after there is a view down into the Barrancos de Marangaño and Bombas de Agua. On past the Degollado de las Palomas the path continues to **Roque Palmero**, 2310m, which is avoided to the right. Yet another hollow (Barranco de Tajodeque) and then the **Morro Pinos Gachos**, 2179m, is reached.

Now the path goes down more steeply to the Hoya del Estrabito, a beautiful little viewpoint at the beginning of the ridge, which is now covered in pines, and which leads over to the summit rise of Somada Alta. The path skirts to the right of the ridge, which drops away steeply to the Caldera. At the end of this long drawn-out crest, shortly before the next descent begins, go up without a path to the summit of **Somada Alta**, 1926m (sign on summit).

Shortly before the Somada Alta – the most impressive section of this walk.

50 The Great Caldera circuit – From the Ermita Virgen del Pino to Mirador El Time

Two-day tour over the highest mountain chain on the island

Ermita de la Virgen del Pino – Refugio de la Punta de los Roques – Pico de la Cruz – Roque de los Muchachos – Somada Alta – Mirador El Time

Starting point: Centro de Visitantes, 870m, on the main road from El Paso – Santa Cruz (bus stop for bus 1).

Destination: Mirador El Time, 510m, on the main road Los Llanos – Puntagorda (bus stop for bus 5).

Walking time: Centro de Visitantes – Pico de la Cruz 7¾ hrs, Pico de la Cruz – Mirador El Time 8¼ hrs, total time 16 hrs.

Ascent: On the first day around 1700m of ascent with only a slight amount of descent, on the second day about 250m of ascent and 2050m of descent (2000m of ascent and 2250m of descent in total).

Grade: This two-day circuit requires an extremely good level of fitness (massive height gain and height loss) as well as sure-footedness and a head for heights, but is only of moderate difficulty. The white-red marked path is always clear and is generally also well sign-posted.

Refreshment and accommodation: Refreshment is only possible at the starting point (Bar-Restaurant Las Piedras) and at the end (Bar-Restaurant El Time). It is therefore necessary to take all the necessary provisions for 2 days, including at least 3 litres of water (no springs en route, a possible well at the Refugio de la Punta and perhaps water at the observatories). There is only a refuge hut en route, the Refugio de la Punta de los Roques, which is, however, too close to the start and would only come into consideration if the walk was spread over 3 days. An overnight stop at the Pico de la Cruz is best (the hut here is locked and serves as a measuring station).

Emergency descent: Between Pico de la Nieve and Roque de los Muchachos it is possible at practically any point in less than an hour to descend to the road (little used and not at all at night) from Santa Cruz to Muchachos – Hoya Grande (no bus connection).

Alternatives: A more difficult walk would be a combination of the Great Caldera Walk with the Volcano Walk (Walk 33) a splendid 3-day walk (second overnight stop, best at the Refugio El Pilar or the Refugio de la Punta de los Roques). Of course, at Mirador del Time it would be possible to add on a descent to Puerto de Tazacorte (Walk 27). From Pico de la Cruz it is possible to descend to Los Sauces (Walk 46) from Mirador de Taburiente there is a possible descent to Roque Faro (Walk 47) from Torre del Time it is possible to descend to La Punta (Walk 26). Almost all of the different sections of the Caldera Circuit can be done as single day walks (Walks 42, 43, 44, 45, 48, 49 and 26).

Important advice: This walk should only be done in settled weather conditions in the summer months – in winter there is mostly snow and correspondingly low temperatures (below zero) to be reckoned with. In any case a bivouac sack/sleeping bag and a foam mat are needed: nights above 2000m are noticeably cold even in summer. Warm clothing and protection from the rain as well as sufficient provisions for 2 days (water!) are an obvious requirement.

This circuit of the Caldera ridge, which requires two full days, can without exaggeration be described as the outstanding walk of the island: no less

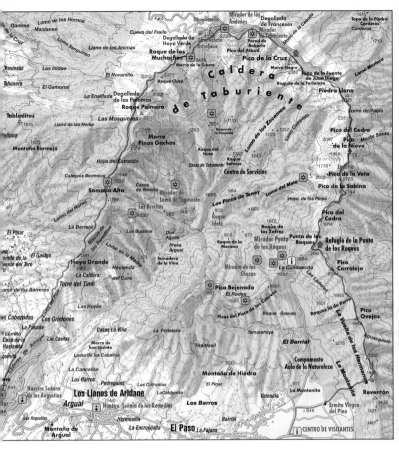

than seven summits of the Grand Caldera circuit are taken in. The walk does however require a very high level of fitness and high mountain experience. As there is no hut for an overnight stay, the walk should only be undertaken in the summer months. A night under what is possibly the clearest sky in Europe, in the immediate vicinity of the observatories and with a fantastic view over large sections of the island, in particular of the Caldera, are the highlights of this megatour.

Follow the road that forks off in the direction of Cumbrecita from the **Centro de Visitantes** and after 1km the road that goes off right to **Ermita Virgen del Pino** (½ hr). From here follow →Walk 29 to the **Reventón Pass**, 1410m

169

Twilight on the Pico de la Cruz.

(good 1 hr), and the white-red marked path to **Refugio de la Punta de los Roques**, 2040m (2½ hrs; →Walk 42). On past the Punta de los Roques the path changes over to the right side of the crest and dips down to the Degollada del Río (sign, 25 min; directly at the beginning of an unpleasant scree descent a small spring basin in a rock niche just above the path, but usually dried up in summer). A good three quarters of an hour later – after a more strenuous ascent the path goes comfortably along the ridge top – the Pico de la Veta de la Arena with the Guanche Gathering Place, La Erita (pre-historic rock engravings) is skirted to the left (rather precipitous section; it is also possible to stay along the crest). Shortly after, the Degollada del Barranco de la Madera (sign) is passed. Two forks in the path are reached in quick succession: in each case go left (descent possible to the Nieve Pista on the right, sign). Then the signposted turning off to the summit of **Pico de la Nieve**, 2239m, is reached (2 hrs from the Refugio de la Punta de los Roques). Now continue as for →Walk 45 to **Pico de la Cruz**, 2351m (1¾ hrs). One should look for a place to sleep in one of the coarsely grained sandy rock niches below the summit hut, which serves as a measuring station.

From Pico de la Cruz continue along the ridge path (do not go off right towards the road after a few minutes), which eventually joins the High Road. A few minutes later the **Mirador de Taburiente** (Degollada de Franceses) is reached. From here follow →Walk 48 to the **Roque de Muchachos**, 2426m (2½ hrs from Pico de la Cruz). Now follow →Walk 49 to the **Somada Alta**, 1926m (2¼ hrs). The walk now continues downwards switching continuously between steeper and easier sections, mainly to the side of the ridge top. After three quarters of an hour – shortly before this the cliff of the Risco de las Pareditas (sign) is passed – a path goes off right to El Jésus. However, keep on along the ridge in the direction of Torre del Time, which leads through the slopes of Hoya Grande. Finally the first garden terraces above the west coast are reached. Keeping left a track is met, which also keeps to the left and leads to the fire observation tower of the **Torre del Time**, 1160m. Then go along the precipitous edge of the ridge which leads to the Angustias Gorge (1½ hrs from Somada Alta). Go past the tower and continue down the track for a good 5 minutes until in a right-hand bend a wide path bordered by stonewalls leads straight on down. This soon leads to the edge of the ridge, but this is left again immediately (watch out for cairns). The path, which is a bit overgrown in places, leads slightly leftwards down to a small pine wood and finally joins a pipe at a gravel track (¾ hr from tower). Immediately a wide unsurfaced road is joined and this is followed to the left (do not turn off right) to its end at the radio station RTVE. From here go along the path near the ridge as far as a reservoir. Now go right down the path, which immediately goes around below to the right of a private plot and meets a track below the houses. In the following right-hand bend the track is left for a path which goes straight onwards back to the edge of the ridge (water pipe on supports, small white »summit cross« on the left). The nearby **Mirador del Time**, 510m, can be reached either by going on along the ridge path or along the paved path, which leads left to the main road (along this to the right in 5 min to Mirador El Time; 2 hrs from Torre del Time).

The morning sun puts the path to Roque de los Muchachos in the right light.

Index